Explorations in Theol

*Explorations in Theology 3*

# J. L. HOULDEN

SCM PRESS LTD

334 01973 7

First published 1978
by SCM Press Ltd
58 Bloomsbury Street, London WC1

Phototypeset in V.I.P. Palatino by
Western Printing Services Ltd, Bristol
and printed in Great Britain by Billing & Sons Ltd,
Guildford, London and Worcester

# Contents

*To Kenneth Woollcombe,*
*with affection*

# Preface & Acknowledgments

The essays collected in this book are all on doctrinal subjects. They are arranged topically rather than chronologically, starting with more fundamental matters and moving on to the eucharist and the church's ministry. The sermon on humility makes a suitable conclusion.

The date of original publication is given in the list of contents. I am grateful to the editors and publishers concerned for permission to reprint essays whose original place of appearance is noted below:

'The Bible and the Faith' from *Catholic Anglicans Today*, ed. John Wilkinson, Darton, Longman & Todd 1968.

'The Doctrine of the Trinity and the Person of Christ' from *The Church Quarterly Review* (published by SPCK), vol. CLXIX, January-March 1968.

'The Place of Jesus' from *What about the New Testament?*, ed. Morna Hooker and Colin Hickling, SCM Press 1975.

'The Idea of the Church' from *Faith and Unity* (published by the Church Union), vol. XVII, July 1973.

'Good Liturgy or even Good Battlefield?' from *Theology* (published by SPCK), vol. LXIX, October 1966.

'Sacrifice and the Eucharist' from *Thinking about the Eucharist*, ed. I. T. Ramsey, SCM Press 1972.

'Liturgy and her Companions' from *The Eucharist Today*, ed. R. C. D. Jasper, SPCK 1974.

'Priesthood' from *Lambeth Essays on Ministry*, ed. A. M. Ramsey, SPCK 1969.

'The Worth of Arguments' from *Women Priests? Yes - Now!*, ed. Harold Wilson, National Christian Education Council 1975.

'On the Grace of Humility' from *Theology*, vol. LXXIX, July 1976.

The two last essays are reproduced in their original, fuller form, and the latter, an Oxford University sermon preached on 29 February 1976, receives its original title. It concludes with some lines from William Plomer's poem 'A Church in Bavaria', from *Celebrations*, which are printed here by permission of the Estate of William Plomer, and Jonathan Cape Ltd.

My thanks are due to John Bowden, editor of SCM Press, for his ready help; to those who noticed and discussed some of these essays when they first appeared, including two doctors of divinity who visited me to remonstrate over 'The Doctrine of the Trinity and the Person of Christ' and another who initiated friendship by appreciating it, and Tom Baker, the Dean of Worcester, who pleased me by referring to 'The Worth of Arguments' as 'characteristically cross-bench'; and to Peter Strange, a faithful and persistent proof-reader.

*Cuddesdon*                                                               J.L.H.
*August 1977*

# *Introduction*

At first sight there could be nothing simpler than assembling pieces written over the years for a variety of purposes and re-issuing them between a single pair of covers. But consider what is involved.

In the first place, the essays are extracted from their original settings and compelled to cohabit merely because they share authorship. Yet the setting is part of the meaning, especially when the essay first appeared alongside others on similar themes, contributing to a whole. This makes for a degree of distortion, though other features compensate; a single mind is disclosed, and in the present case it is seen at work on a series of doctrinal themes – the area of interest is intelligibly de-limited.

In the second place, essays are random samples of a person's thoughts over the period covered by their composition, in this case about a decade. Some will be the result of more prolonged thought than others, but none is likely to give more than a glimpse into the writer's mind. They are peaks jutting above the clouds. The solid structure of his development and of what he 'really means' lies hidden.

This is true in two senses. First, essays are disconnected pieces, produced at intervals, often *ad hoc*; so there are gaps in the chain, not always easy to fill in by guesswork. The reader sees only a mind flitting from one topic to another, haphazardly. Second, there is a reverse side to any man's non-autobiographical writ-ings which is part (but only part) of the key to comprehending them. He writes on a theme, whether allotted to him or by choice, and he states the truth he sees; but an inner self prods and pushes the pen, often largely unawares. Deep assumptions cannot be explored every time he sits down to write. Guiding ideas and characteristics need to be unearthed if the writings are to be understood with sympathy; and perhaps the joy of reading vol-umes of essays lies precisely in detecting symptoms of another

man's view of the world and (with luck) revelling in its strangeness.

In the case of a collection of essays, this factor has added
interest. If they were written over a number of years, they may
well reflect substantial inner development, perhaps radical shifts
of outlook, achieved during the period. Unless such shifts are
quirky, they are likely to be of interest because they correspond
sufficiently to what others have undergone or may be ready to
undergo. And even when they arouse dissent, at least it is likely
to be a more understanding dissent when engaged at this level
than when it is concerned with the outward manifestations
alone, that is, the essays regarded as visible peaks.

In this present collection, one essay is crucial from this point of
view. More than a mere isolated peak, it is an important part of
the terrain itself. It is not just a symptom of ideas chiefly felt and
developed elsewhere: its writing was a major step in my growth
(less than original though I subsequently found it to be). 'The
Doctrine of the Trinity and the Person of Christ' was composed
for a relaxed Oxford after-dinner theological society (and how
heavy it was for the purpose!). At the time, it worked *itself* out and
its significance was quite lost on me. Looking back, I see that it
was more important to me for its method and approach than for
its content. It was a movement towards a step which must be
taken: the application to doctrinal ideas of that historical and
analytical criticism which is generally accepted in relation to the
Bible. More widely: nothing expressed in words can be exempt
from the limiting conditions of historical setting, and 'time-
lessness' is a chimera. Better, the limitations give ideas their
flavour and their opportunity; they are the conditions of life. One
essay ('Good Liturgy or even Good Battlefield?') antedates the
achieving of this perspective – and some readers may find it the
only tolerable piece in the book! I now find it lacking in analytical
depth. It does not go to the roots and its perspective is wrong.

Most of these essays are concerned with subjects less close to
the centre of Christian faith than the Trinity and the person of
Christ. They are in the realm of applied doctrine – church, eucharist, ministry; areas where the vicissitudes of history and society
bear more obviously on the formulation of faith and where the
practical, institutional element is inescapable. But the method
and approach to which I refer find themselves penetrating
everywhere.

Three concerns have been borne in upon me over the years

covered by these essays. They lie behind the theological problems at which most of them are worrying. First, the need for this kind of historical and analytical approach if we are to make realistic and sympathetic assessments of doctrine. How it could sweeten controversy and transform ecumenical negotiations! Without it a complete dimension required for understanding is missing; for if we deal merely with words, not enquiring who speaks them, and when, and where, we have an impossibly rigid basis for seeing what is meant. Certainly, love is unlikely to grow.

Second, the need to investigate the relationship between Christian statement in the 'applied' areas and on more fundamental matters, and to ensure that the relationship is kept close and consistent. Christian faith is a seamless robe; yet how easily it is split into parts, and how readily conclusions in one are at variance with conclusions in another.

The third is the attempt to move as far as possible away from technical and into 'plain' language, an attempt not always appreciated. Thus, the essay on 'Priesthood' was, I heard, criticized when it first appeared for failing to state the doctrine of the indelibility of orders. It appears to me to be nothing else than an attempt to put the considerations involved in that traditional doctrine in language which is both non-technical and related to the observable truth about the ministry in the church.

It is harder to say why any of these objectives is worth pursuing. In a sense, I seek them because they impose themselves; other ways seem to lack candour and penetration, to be increasingly artificial and unsatisfactory. They seem to impose themselves – and that may be all and sufficient. But I think they do so because of an underlying conviction that Christian faith is not esoteric and is capable of communication in language accessible to those who will attend. Esotericism arises when styles of discussion once current or current elsewhere are preserved and insisted on in quite different cultural settings, where only extreme effort or self-exclusion from common understanding and common questioning can ensure their survival. The essay about the ordination of women ('The Worth of Arguments') is a tour de force, illustrating briskly and bluntly a number of these considerations. It had to be written in haste one August morning: the need for rapid action gave it a rough clarity which might merit some apology if it did not have the advantage of showing my hand. The essay on 'Sacrifice and the Eucharist' (a lightning tour if ever there was one) demonstrates the force of some of the same points.

The approach taken here has its place in relation to the present state of theology in the church. The church is now a minority in society; Christian theology is one voice among many within general thought. It is wholly to be expected that the church should find itself pressed into increasing concern with its own domestic affairs, and that its theological interest should concentrate on internal matters of structure and discipline. Two of the essays in this book ('Sacrifice and the Eucharist' and 'Liturgy and her Companions') were written as contributions to collections sponsored by the Liturgical and Doctrine Commissions of the Church of England, much of whose time has been devoted to matters of this kind.

One result of this situation is that 'theology' comes to signify two quite distinct clusters of issues, increasingly polarized, often attracting the interest of distinct groups. Within the church's official agenda, matters like the ordination of women and marriage discipline assume a central place. Report of their treatment, however, serves only to make the church seem more and more alien to those outside an inner circle, and is incapable of creating or warming faith. On the wider scene, fundamental issues like the worthwhileness of religious concern, the being and character of God, and the sense in human life in a problematic world present themselves with urgency: *they* are what theology is about. Overwhelmingly, the need for theological and evangelistic effort lies here, and by comparison other matters seem trivial. One may even not know how to take them seriously as fit matters of theological interest.

Meanwhile (it is another effect of the church's present position), attempts to re-examine traditional questions in the light of our circumstances can reliably expect from many of the faithful much more alarm and wrath than gratitude or even tolerant interest. The faith is seen as a fortress to the defence of whose ramparts we must continually rush, not a body of people entering delightedly upon ever-new lands, laid before us by the Creator of all good.

Many of the essays in this book deal with subjects which on this account must be described as ecclesiastical. But they attempt to do it from a point of view which is not merely domestic; and the hope is to create a better sense of proportion in these matters, so that they may be seen more easily in relation to the central questions which merit so much more of our attention.

The sermon 'On the Grace of Humility' has a message which

suitably rounds off the collection. Christian faith and prayer, not controversy, are the chief concern of these essays. It is a great thing to dare to speak about God. Misplaced confidence in our words is as big a danger in Christian theology as silence – and far commoner. The overriding need to speak of God, though fearfully, is the motive for the twin concern for simplicity of language and consistency of statement. Theology is always about God; and if it seems to be about the eucharist or the Jesus of history or liberation in South America, then it is only in so far as they reflect God or God bears on them. The essence of such an approach, as far as words are concerned, is a continual dissatisfaction. There is no verbal resting-place in the quest for God or his quest for us. Exploration is unremitting.

Much Christian theology is then properly critical. In this mood, it aims not to state truth about God so much as to assess statements about him: expose their cultural, social and intellectual pedigree; demonstrate what they are able to say and what they cannot say. Most of these essays belong in that category. They exemplify a method and an attitude, born partly of this style of Christian conviction, partly of the force of the evidence. To give greater – or, better, a different kind of – weight to Christian statements, however venerable, and to ignore the findings and attitudes of modern historical method is not only to fail in ordinary intellectual integrity but also to approach too close to the Burning Bush.

Nevertheless, the Voice has spoken and requires us to persist – not just in critical theology but in speech which is by way of response. This speech consists of both the clearest statement we can find concerning God and speech towards God. Theology is one means of attempting alert obedience to God through Christ who brought him near to our eyes.

# 1

## *The Bible and the Faith*

There has never been a time when the Bible has been more attractively, conveniently and painlessly presented for the Christian's use than the present. Translations into brave attempts at contemporary English appear constantly. Editions with helpful notes by distinguished experts and series of commentaries designed for every shade of competence abound. Yet despite all, the dish often fails to satisfy, and gives rise to unease. Of course sometimes (and for many Christians nearly always) it does nothing of the sort; it is still simply the pure milk of the Word. But this is because they impose limitations which for others have proved impossible and even undesirable. They use the Bible largely or exclusively as the basis for prayer and the means of edification; and often in practice they attend chiefly to those parts of it which lend themselves most naturally to this purpose. The disquiet arises when the Bible is used in other ways, when questions of other kinds are raised, and when the Bible as a whole is opened for frank examination. Then, modern translations and useful notes, far from finally answering questions, merely pose them more acutely and lead on to others more far-reaching. The strangeness of the cultures lying behind the biblical documents, problems of historicity and the sheer unwieldy bulk of the books all force themselves upon the attention. In other words, all the questions which arise when modern skills are applied to these books, and modern interests (e.g. historical or anthropological investigation) are brought to bear upon them impose themselves all the more stridently.

Catholic Christians have sometimes felt a certain detachment from these questions. Their emphasis on the tradition of the church as authenticating doctrine and their strong dependence upon the sacraments in practical devotion have relieved the anxiety which a more exclusive reliance upon scripture might have generated. Such relief has perhaps been dearly bought and may be psychologically helpful more than it is rationally respectable, for in the structure of the faith, changing attitudes to, and any new questions about, the Bible are equally important for Christians of all traditions. Nevertheless in some ways, a Christian of a Catholic outlook ought to find himself predisposed to understand the perspectives opened up by fresh approaches to the Bible. In particular, in the light of his strong church-awareness, he will not find it hard to see that the biblical documents themselves, from first to last, are the product of a society or community sharing a certain outlook of faith, and do not exist in their own independent right. Nor will he find it hard to see that this community is a changing thing, sharing in a constant succession of cultures, and that the biblical books have their roots in these varied settings and are formed by them. He will no doubt be daunted by the sheer weight and complexity of modern biblical scholarship, but its basic modes of operation should cause little searching of heart.

It is not our purpose to attempt a survey of the many questions raised for the believer by modern attitudes to the Bible. The literature on that subject is enormous in volume and of high quality. We confine ourselves to an area often neglected but of great importance for the Christian who sees that faith depends not only upon the Bible but upon the work of the Spirit in the church as an articulate society. It is the delicate and complex matter of the relationship of the Bible with the church's faith.

The New Testament documents spring from the believing and worshipping church. They fix the faith and adoration of the church in words, according to certain specific literary forms (like epistle, gospel and apocalypse), and, at the time of their writing, according to the needs and conceptions of certain specific circumstances (those of Paul and his audience, or Matthew and the church for which he wrote). But once they have come into existence, they begin to acquire authority, at first only locally and in small degree. From that moment, these fixed forms of words not only express faith but also mould it. Faith itself continues: held in environments increasingly removed from those out of which these books came. The books travel and are brought to bear upon that faith in senses remote from their original purpose. The church in Alexandria reads the epistles to the Corinthians in the light of its own faith, its own thought-forms and its own problems; and while certainly allowing its own way of thinking of the faith to be affected by them cannot attempt to simulate the prob-

lems and ideas of Corinth years before. So an interchange is
inaugurated which continues from that day to this, between the
documents, increasingly authoritative, first formed *by* the
church, then data *for* the church, and the faith as held by those
receiving the documents. This relationship is one of infinite complexity and shifts continually; for though the documents remain
the same, they are read by ever-changing eyes.

Our task is to examine some aspects of this interchange and to
try and see how it works. How does Christian doctrine emerge
from scripture? Or, if this is not the right question (in that the
New Testament itself expresses already existing faith), how is
doctrine related to scripture? What exactly is happening when
appeal is made to scripture, either in general or to particular texts,
in support of a doctrine? Does the producing of a biblical text in
any way clinch a doctrinal argument, and if so, why? To what
extent should a Christian seeking authority for a belief or a
practice, look first for a biblical text and regard his search as likely
to end in settling the matter, one way or the other? And if this
procedure seems crude and unsatisfactory, what alternative is
there? To appeal to biblical themes? But they too are not easy to
disentangle, for the Bible does not seem to speak with a single
voice.

In practice, such questions as these are most likely to be
answered with the New Testament in mind. But there was a time,
a considerable period of about two centuries, when the church
did not possess a 'New Testament' as an authoritative collection
of books, but simply a series of writings and groups of writings
(like the letters of Paul) which were gradually acquiring the status
of a fixed and authoritative collection. We shall begin by going
back to that period, when 'scripture' meant simply the Old
Testament, taken over by the church from Judaism, and we shall
see whether the situation of the church at that time casts any light
upon our questions. From the literature of that period, in fact
from the time when the later books of the New Testament were
being written, there is a passage in a letter of Ignatius, bishop of
Antioch, dated about AD 112, which will give us a useful start.

He writes to the church in Philadelphia, where dissident
groups are appealing to the Old Testament in support of posi-
tions which they have adopted.

> I urge you, do not do things in cliques, but act as Christ's disciples.
> When I heard some people saying, 'If I don't find it in the original
> documents, I don't believe it in the gospel,' I answered them, 'But it *is*

written there.' They retorted, 'That's just the question.' To my mind it is Jesus Christ who is the original documents. The inviolable archives are his cross and death and resurrection and the faith that came by him.[1]

However much or little Ignatius, writing on the eve of his martyrdom, saw in these words, both the distinction which he draws and the principle which he erects have vast implications for Christian faith. The 'original documents' are the books of the Old Testament, and with them he contrasts 'Christ', and he goes on to 'unpack' that name to mean 'his cross and death and resurrection and the faith that came by him.' It is a question of which is to be the measure of the other: the old or the new.

We are fortunate to have this brief glimpse of Christian minds at work on this question at a most interesting moment in Christian development. It is enough to enable us to use it as a specimen, presenting in a relatively simple form several problems with which Christian doctrine perennially faces us.

In the first place, what, more precisely, is in question? In a rough way, no doubt Ignatius and those to whom he writes were at one in affirming the scriptural status of the Old Testament: they accepted it as authoritative for Christians. They differed in the way they saw this authority working. Any reasonable man will readily admit that the Old Testament presents formidable difficulties if it is to be used as a basis for belief. As a way of entering into an understanding of Judaism or of Israel's history and institutions over a very long period, it is indispensable. As a way of getting the feel of a response to God which is (considering the great length of the period involved) amazingly consistent, it is incomparable. But as a document of authoritative doctrine it looks both inefficient and risky. How should one set about using this vast collection of writings for such a purpose? Even to a reader like Ignatius and his contemporaries, much less sensitive than we are to their shifting historical background, product of more than a millennium, they all too clearly lack the handiness of a creed, the considered clarity of a set of conciliar decrees. It is no wonder that even by the time of Ignatius, when the church was not yet a century old, there was room for disagreement and uncertainty. There was no universally agreed or obvious way for Christians to handle the Old Testament.

The truth is that the church had already (it is clear from the New Testament writings, mostly in existence by this time) produced a set of quite disparate answers to the crucial question of its relation to its Jewish heritage, and to the Old Testament in particular, not all of them equally satisfactory from a doctrinal point of view. These answers were not fully worked out, not wholly conscious, and certainly the disparity between them was not clearly perceived. They jostled side by side in writings of various kinds, in Christian prayer and discourse. All of them served as principles of selection for Christian writers as they sought to give an account of the Old Testament basis for Christian faith. We shall distinguish three of these answers and estimate their value for understanding and formulating Christian doctrine.

1. Many Christians in the second century still saw the division between the church and Judaism as far from absolute. The church was the new Israel, in unbroken development from the old. She was the true inheritor of the promises, the life and the institutions of Israel. At the end of the second century, Christians in North Africa were buying their meat from the kosher butchers, and in the fourth century at Antioch there was intense devotion in the church to the martyrs of the Maccabean revolt of the second century BC. To this day, an Ethiopian Christian observes the Jewish food laws, keeps Sabbath as well as Sunday and circumcises his male offspring. This view regards persisting Jews as either apostates or, more gently, erring brothers. It is of course entirely comprehensible: the church began, in an age of many Jewish sects, as one such sect among others. It is not unfair to define the church of the first years as the group of Jews who believed that Jesus of Nazareth was the promised Messiah of God. Even the incorporation of Gentiles on generous terms did not go beyond some Old Testament prophecies and the hopes of many Jews, particularly those living outside Palestine in the cities of the Mediterranean world.

In this view, the stress is on two features which have an undoubted place in a final picture but, as we shall see, do not merit such a dominating one. The first feature is continuity; the second, Israel as the people of God. The new Israel succeeds to the old, and essentially the two are one. If the logic of this view is pursued, it is clear that the role of Jesus is minimal. He is simply the one who stands at the parting of the ways, where the church continues the main line of development and Judaism disappears down a false trail. His life is an incident, however important an incident, in the history of Israel, which is the continuing entity. It is of course true that this view is rarely held in isolation, but it constitutes one identifiable strand in Christian thinking and devotion which is not always set in relation to other more satisfactory ways of expression. In a diagram, it looks like this:

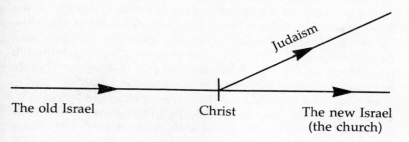

The old Israel       Christ       The new Israel (the church)

2. A second view places less value on continuity, much more on the parallelism between old and new. But while showing that each element in the life and institutions of the church has a counterpart in the old Israel which foreshadowed it, this view is clear about the superiority of the new and about the distinction between it and the old. Nevertheless, taken by itself, it provides no clear way of deciding what in the Old Testament is of Christian value, apart from the mere fact that a plausible parallel is discernible in the arrangements of the church. Thus, it so happens that Sunday is the parallel in the life of the church to Sabbath in the life of Israel, in the sense that each is the specially observed day of the week in the society in question: but it is hard to see any intrinsic doctrinal reason why there should be in old Israel such an equivalent to the Christian institution, if that should be taken as the datum, or why the reverse should be true, if one looks at it the other way round.

Moreover, the role of Jesus is even more incidental in this second scheme than in the first. It is true that he stands between old and new, and alone gives rise to the new, but he plays no really vital part in the logic of the scheme itself, for it is chiefly concerned with the parallelism between two sets of religious institutions and ideas and with the items of equipment which each set possesses. It is almost as if there were an inventory of kit which 'a religion' ought to have; and clearly in theory one could make a similar comparison between the Old Testament religion and any other religion that one cared to select. There is nothing in the logic of the pattern to demand that the church be seen as *the* place where the true counterparts are to be found.

At the very least, this view has an undoubted place in Christian edification. It is devotionally helpful to see Jesus as a new Moses or a new David, to see Easter as a new Passover, baptism as the Red Sea crossing for each of us. The question is whether it can be trusted to roam unchecked in areas where Christian *doctrine* is being formulated. In the New Testament and in the early church generally, nobody was much disposed to distinguish sharply between the writing of devotional literature and theology, and in many ways this was salutary. But when it comes to stating doctrine clearly, the effect can easily be unfortunate. The helpful analogy is elevated to the status of theological statement, and is unable to sustain the role.

It is not difficult to find more examples of this model. Baptism is the counterpart not only of the crossing of the Red Sea at the exodus but also of the rite of circumcision; the eucharist parallels the Jewish sacrifices, the Christian priesthood the Aaronic, a Christian emperor one of the pious kings of Judah. In each case, so far as this view is concerned, though the Christian is in no doubt that the new supersedes the old, in fact the stress is on what the two parallel institutions share. This obscures the newness of the Christian institution and the differentiating features of both. Thus, when baptism and circumcision are set side by side, what really makes the parallelism work is the fact that they both fall into the category: 'rite of initiation into the people of God'. This, however, by no means exhausts the meaning of either rite, and, as far as baptism is concerned, it fails to draw attention to its chief significance as the rite of entry into relationship with Christ, or to its organic connection with the central facts of the gospel. Seeing its biblical basis in relation to the Jewish rite has in fact served to obscure the most important things which Christian doctrine has to say about it. Exactly the same situation arises with regard to sacrifice and priesthood, which, while they may bring out certain important ideas about the eucharist and the Christian ministry, all too easily obscure more important ones which relate them directly to the core of the gospel.

Before we leave the example of baptism in relation to this scheme of thought, we ought to examine the other Old Testament counterpart to which we referred, the crossing of the Red Sea by Israel at the exodus. Here, the common element which leads to the choice of this event as significant is not, as in the case of circumcision, baptism's function as the rite of initiation, but rather the idea of deliverance from the old life of sin and death (= Egypt and the life of slavery to which Israel was subjected there) into the new life of freedom in Christ (= the promised land which lay, in due course, on the far side of the Red Sea). But even more important for the imaginative and devotional usefulness of this parallel from the Old Testament has been the fact that both in it and in baptism water figured prominently. For the proper understanding of Christian baptism in relation to the central insights of the gospel, even for its proper understanding in relation to a whole long sequence of God's saving acts in which the exodus is seen to have an important place, this fact is totally fortuitous. Yet it is easy for it to draw attention away from central considerations to ideas which, though devotionally rich, are doctrinally peripheral. It makes for a neat and elegant pattern, and is soon regarded as a providential gift for theology.

Put in a diagram, the second view appears thus:

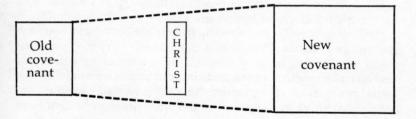

Here, the new is certainly more than *merely* parallel to the old: it supersedes and transcends it. But essentially it does no more than reproduce it. Because the old comes first, in effect it calls the tune, determining what is seen as really significant in the new, and exerting pressure in the direction of Judaizing the new. Moreover, though Christ certainly stands between the two, the lines connecting them just fail to go through him.

3. When it is a matter of framing Christian doctrine, no scheme will be fully satisfactory that does not have Christ at its centre; and not just formally so, as in the two diagrams above, but structurally, integrally so. He must be the lynch-pin of the whole pattern, indispensable to its existence and coherence, and vitally affecting each part of it. The following diagram expresses this

conviction, as far as the relation of the Old Testament to the Christian dispensation is concerned:

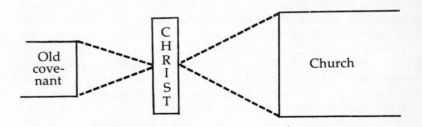

In this diagram, all the lines which join the church to the Old Testament pass through Christ, and he alone makes the contact possible. The positive values of the other two schemes (in the first case, continuity, in the second, parallelism) are preserved, but in a new setting. What the diagram does not make clear is the exact nature of Christ's mediating position. In fact, it is a double role: he is both selector and transformer.

First, he selects. Not everything in the Old Testament is grist to the mill of Christian doctrine. It is no doubt true that we must study the Old Testament as a whole if we want to get a balanced and complete picture of the formation of Judaism; true also that Jesus sprang from that process. But that is not our present concern. What interests us here is neither what Judaism in the time of Jesus was like nor what the historical Jesus was like, but the doctrinal significance of Christ for the church and her gospel and the way the expression of that significance is related to the Old Testament background, when the Old Testament is regarded as authoritative scripture. We repeat: Christ selects from the Old Testament certain images and insights at the expense of others. For example, the idea of 'Christ' (Messiah) itself receives, when attached to Jesus, a significance much greater than its rather meagre occurrence in the Old Testament would suggest; while the crudely nationalistic strain which is prominent in many parts of the Old Testament is abandoned or treated in a purely figurative way.

The process of selection also has the effect of bringing together themes and images which were not connected at all in the Old Testament: e.g. Jesus appears as both Messiah and Suffering Servant (cf. Isa. 53), as Second Adam (I Cor. 15.22) and as New

Moses (II Cor. 3.7-15). It is true that, in their background in ancient Israelite thought and imagery, some of these figures were probably connected with each other, but these links are not at all explicit in the Old Testament itself. The images come together only because they throw light on the significance of Jesus.

Jesus not only selects; he also transforms. In other words, he is not controlled by the images and insights which he derives from the Old Testament, but himself controls them. This control is exercised not only over the actual using of an image or idea but also over its meaning. To take an example, the sense in which messiahship is attributed to Jesus is different from its use in popular Judaism. In the straightforward sense he does not correspond to what ordinary Jews expected of the promised great king who would deliver Israel from its oppressors. In the gospel of St John, the suffering and death of Jesus are portrayed in regal terms, to make clear the conviction that Jesus was never so truly king as when, to the ordinary observer, he looked least like it. We might be inclined to describe this change as a 'spiritualizing' of the concept of Messiah: Jesus is not a king like Augustus or David or Herod, but a 'sort-of-king' to those who accept his teaching. But this is not quite adequate, because there issues from him a society, the church, which is identifiable, with membership and organization, and in which his rule is accepted in all areas of life. And the cross remains the sharpest expression of his rule. The result is that we are led to redefine the whole notion of *rule* (implicit in messiahship) in terms of generous self-giving and service. Because his authority is exercised in this way and has these characteristics, the community which stems from him came to see such authority as the ideal for its own life and conduct. The concept has not only been selected from the Old Testament but also transformed by its application to Jesus.

Putting this in another way, we can say that the idea of Messiah in the Old Testament is useful and important for Christian doctrine only because it has been selected by Christ and only as it has been transformed by him, above all by his death. It has, that is, no intrinsic right to a place in the pattern. Its place is given and determined by Christ. The same is true of all other Old Testament concepts and institutions which find an echo or a replica in the Christian dispensation. Thus, it may well be the case, as many Christians have held from the first century, that the sacrifices of the Old Testament provide a doctrinal background to the Christian eucharist and the Old Testament priesthood to the Christian clergy. But if this is to be so, one essential condition has to be fulfilled, that is, that the argument has to work according to our third diagram and not according to our second. In other words, any usefulness which this background has is wholly subordinate to the central data concerning Christ. If the imagery of sacrifice helpfully illuminates the meaning of the eucharist, as expressing liturgically the Christians' relationship to God through Christ, then it has a valid place in doctrinal statement. Otherwise, though it may have a place in the more freely imaginative language of devotion, its presence in doctrinal patterns will merely mislead. The first kind of statement will, after all, always be optional, for the use of those who find it religiously helpful; the second ought to aim at more careful expression which will command wide acceptance.

The model illustrated in our third diagram applies not only to biblical images like messiahship or institutions like sacrifice, but also to great all-embracing biblical themes such as 'covenant' or 'righteousness' and to far-reaching characteristics of biblical thought like eschatology. In cases like these, it is easy to stress the continuity between the Old Testament and Christian doctrine. In both (if we take the example of eschatology), God is seen as acting in history towards determined ends. In both it is right to describe his purpose as ultimately redemptive. But here too, Christ transforms. For the New Testament writers, the object of God's redemptive purpose is not precisely what it was in the Old Testament. Its defining lines are set by the life, death and resurrection of Jesus, and he himself appears as embodying that purpose, initiating its realization among men. The Old Testament provides analogies and directions for thought, but could not of itself lead us to guess the place to which they would lead.

When Ignatius found it necessary to correct the Philadelphians' use of the Old Testament, we do not know what sort of argument they had been putting forward. It may have been something corresponding to either of our first two models; it may have been a quite simple appeal to Old Testament law as still binding upon Christians (presupposing diagram 1), or what was in effect a Judaizing of some Christian idea or institution (diagram 2). In any case, in repudiating their views, Ignatius appeals to our third model. It is Christ alone who is the selector and controller of Old Testament images and ideas as they pass into the Christian church for doctrinal use. The church is to use them in the light of the basic data concerning him as the agent of God's purpose.

It will be clear that there is nothing simple about a claim to derive one's doctrine from the Bible. Up to now, because we took as a specimen a passage from Ignatius, from a time before the New Testament had been assembled or recognized, we have been seeing what happens when the Old Testament is used as source or backing for Christian doctrine. We need to go on to see how the New Testament affects the picture; but before that, there are one or two elaborations to be made to the argument we have already presented.

We look again briefly at the three thought-models illustrated in the diagrams. There is no difficulty in seeing that the first of them was bound to be prominent in the church's early days before she became clearly aware of herself as an independent institution. Elements of it survive, especially in liturgy; for example, the *Exultet*, the deacon's proclamation at the Easter Vigil in the Western rite, movingly affirms the continuity of the church with the old Israel and of Easter with the first Passover night (while also owing much to the second model). But we should be wrong to fear that such surviving elements constituted any threat to our proper holding of the faith; the wider context in which they appear always acts as an adequate corrective, in this case the Easter message of our Lord's resurrection itself.

But it would be a mistake to suppose that its distorting influence upon doctrine was confined to the church's first years. When Stuart kings of England identified themselves with the godly kings of Judah like Hezekiah and Josiah and modelled Christian polity on Old Testament precedents, there was a highly significant use of the first model for doctrinal purposes. Its failure to be a permanently valid analysis of the gospel's implications for political life is an indication of the inadequacy of the first model.

Despite examples such as this, no Christian body has ever ordered itself exclusively according to this model, seeing itself as simply 'Judaism with Jesus as the Messiah'. Always in practice, the more important ways of using the Old Testament background have been the second and third models, with the tensions and confusions between them largely unresolved. The main harmful effect of the confusions has been, as we have suggested, to obscure the direct connection of all Christian doctrine with the central facts of the proclamation about Christ and the relationship with God which he opens up for man.

Alongside this source of muddle and partly related to it is another. It concerns not, as in the former case, the criteria for making selection from an unwieldy mass of material, but rather the manner of regarding the matter that is selected. By what analogy are Christians to understand the role of the doctrinally significant parts of the Old Testament? Many Christians have taken them as having the same sort of authority as a legal text: timeless words about which the chief question is that of establishing the right interpretation, there being no question of going behind them to anything else (such as their cultural provenance or the beliefs of the people who produced them). They are simply oracles given to the human race as saving truth: the task of man is to understand them as sheer words, at most to develop their implications.

Sometimes and for some purposes, when this approach has been taken, it has not seemed necessary or desirable even to make selections from the authoritative scripture. When it is a question of supporting or establishing doctrinal tenets it is scarcely avoidable; but when the purpose is shifted or widened to that of using the scripture as from end to end a book of life-giving spiritual truth, then, whatever extravagant interpretations (e.g. reading uncongenial stories as allegories of acceptable truths) may become necessary to render it intelligible, it is possible to see it as 'the interminable monologue of God'[2] – to accept it as sheer words, which are to be savoured and cherished. Between this use of scripture (of which Origen and Augustine were the brilliant exponents, influencing the whole Christian tradition), and its use for strictly doctrinal purposes, the line is often hard to draw, still harder to adhere to firmly.

We referred to the extravagant interpretations to which the Christian interpreter has often resorted in order to make scripture (seen as sheer words) Christianly intelligible. This means, in effect, that he sets up a criterion above scripture in terms of which he judges it: he knows, in approaching scripture, what it must turn out to mean. That criterion is the faith, the doctrine. Often he will not see it in these terms: he will not go through the process of finding that scripture must be interpreted in this elaborate and improbable way in order to make it doctrinally satisfactory. Rather he will say that, whatever the appearances, this is what scripture must be intended to mean, for it must speak with a single voice. Only when historical criticism makes us see what the original writers are likely to have had in mind, and when we see their meaning as *the* meaning, do we find the old exegesis strained or forced and realize that 'the faith', Christian doctrine, has really been in control. Until this happens, it can scarcely be perceived that there are two distinct ways of using scripture as a ground for doctrine: first as oracles, sheer words; second, as a witness, in a wide variety of ways, to what lies behind it, the basic data of the faith, the 'cross and death and resurrection' of Christ.

The two ways lead to quite different conceptions of Christian doctrine as a whole. The first almost always leads in the direction of the itemized, propositional view of doctrine. It is more likely to put forward tenets of faith (e.g. the virgin birth of our Lord or the descent into hell) because they are evidenced in scriptural texts and in the form in which they are scripturally supported rather than because of any necessary coherence with the central Christian data.

According to the second way, doctrine is what the central data lead us to infer about God and his purposes, and it is no more than this. It is, in other words, a homogeneous, consistent articulation of what God has done in Christ, not a series of mysteries or a set of detached articles of belief.

Sometimes there may be a clash between the two ways. The texts may seem to point to a tenet in such a form that it cannot be brought into connection with the central data. It seems not to meet them in any vital way and becomes a doctrinally useless pious curiosity. In such cases, the tenet loses its status as 'doctrine' and must enter some other category: perhaps mere fact of history, perhaps legend. Most often, it will be an edifying story which, in the idiom of some early Christian writer, served as comment on the central data: it is not doctrine but poetic variation upon a doctrinal theme.

Perhaps the simplest way of illustrating the unsatisfactory nature of the first way is to show how it operates in the closely related matter of seeking ethical guidance from the Bible. Faced with a new moral question, Christians turn to the scriptures. The procedure often used could not unfairly be described as ransacking the Bible to discover some incident or statement which could conceivably bear upon the problem. An obvious example is the scriptural sanctioning of the policy of apartheid by the Dutch Reformed Church in South Africa on the basis of ancient stories in Genesis about the relations between peoples formerly inhabiting the Tigris-Euphrates valleys and surrounding areas. It is easy to see how this method can yield results totally out of harmony with the moral implications of the central data of the gospel. The New Testament itself repeatedly shows these to be chiefly love of

God and love of the neighbour, duties taking precedence over all others, and guiding the working out of all others.

By a second route we arrive again at Ignatius' formula; not the documents but Christ, 'his cross and death and resurrection', are the primary authority for doctrine.

In some of our examples, we have already had in mind the whole Bible, but what is the effect of the development which took place after Ignatius' time, the formation of the New Testament canon of scripture?

In our third diagram (p. 14), we left the Old Testament box open on the side pointing away from Christ, in order to suggest that not everything in the Old Testament directly leads to him: he selects and transforms. Though the way of relationship with God which the Old Testament portrays can be said to lead to Christ, so that we say that he 'fulfils' the Old Testament, yet there remains to the end in the Old Testament a certain imprecision and ambiguity which only he resolves. He completes the pattern – but only if it is looked at in a certain way. Only he makes us see it in that certain way. Only Christ himself determines that we give greater significance to this feature rather than that; and to some elements he gives a prominence and clarity which are not found in the Old Testament at all.

In the same diagram, we also left open the 'church' box on the side which looks to the future; but the sense this time is different. The point here is to enable us to distinguish between Christ and the New Testament scriptures which bear witness to him. Those writings themselves lead us to distinguish two levels in the witness they bear. In the first place, they give evidence of a central proclamation of the redemptive acts of God in Christ, a proclamation formulated in a variety of ways but always agreeing on the death and resurrection. This proclamation, the basic Christian data, was from the start the church's *raison d'être*. This she celebrated in her life of charity and in her eucharistic assemblies; this she communicated to all whom she reached; on this basis she planted herself in city after city of the Roman world. We see it in its simplest form in I Cor. 15.3ff., more elaborately in the apostolic speeches in Acts (e.g. 2.14-36; 13.16-41), in poetic liturgical form in Phil. 2.6-11. This proclamation has moulded every writer in the New Testament. Amply witnessed to in those books, it goes on to have a life of its own in the church, even after the New Testament books have been written. It is substantially identical with what the church came to call its 'rule of faith'; it finds concrete expression in forms of words like baptismal creeds, liturgies, material for the instruction of converts, and eventually the formal statements issued by councils of church leaders. Frequently, as would be expected, the *words* used to express it are those of scripture, but the *content* goes behind scripture and is in essence older than even the earliest books of the New Testament.

In the second place, around the central data the New Testament writers have used a wide variety of literary forms with a wide variety of aims. The evangelists, each with the needs of a particular audience in mind, each with his own theological outlook, gave the traditions about Jesus' life and death – not disinterestedly and objectively, but on the basis of the central data, the life, death and resurrection seen as revealing God's purposes and making them effective for man. Paul wrote to Corinth to answer questions and to correct abuses; but he makes his judgments in the light of the basic proclamation. The writer to the Hebrews expounds the central data in his own rich idiom, but still he is addressing a community which faces specific problems and runs certain risks, and these shape his exposition. The Revelation of John sets the central data against a backcloth of the whole cosmic plan of God, but still he writes in order to meet the needs of the seven churches addressed in the second and third chapters.

At both levels there is a meeting of God's acts in Christ with a response from specific elements in the Christian community. The two interact from the first moment of each encounter: the acts cannot be spoken of at all without acquiring the colour of the mind which speaks. Even the simplest statement of all (I Cor. 15.3ff.), which Paul says he inherits from the church before him, is not free from his own typical emphases. Nevertheless, the two sides of the interaction can be distinguished; and clearly they carry different degrees of authority. God's acts are the saving initiative to which faith responds. The response of the primitive church, seen in the New Testament books, is, however edifying, in principle simply a response, like our own. Inasmuch as both are responses to the action of God, we can range ours alongside theirs. The special value of their response as against ours lies in its directness, its immediacy, and its freedom from the accumulations which time loads upon the church's theological tradition. The New Testament gives the inestimable benefit of what we may regard as a set of 'worked examples' of faithful and authentic response to the acts, from the earliest years. The examples are extensive enough to give us the idea of 'how the game works', how, that is, the central data give rise to doctrinal and ethical thinking in the context of human life. The New Testament books fulfil, in other words, for Christian doctrine a function not unlike that of the examples which the writer of a mathematical textbook uses to illustrate a theorem. That is, they enable us to go on and work out our own problems for ourselves by the right methods. If we are wise, we shall constantly refer back to the examples in order to check that we are on the right lines. But there are two things we shall take care not to do: we shall not mistake the examples for the theorem itself; and we shall not suppose that the examples limit the range of the theorem's application. That application will widen indefinitely as we find new practical problems which our principle helps us to solve.

If this analogy holds, it leads us to a view of the authority of scripture which is both strong and creative. The basis of Christian doctrine is twofold: the redeeming acts of God in Christ, and the continuing relationship with God which those acts establish for man. The Old Testament provides both the basic religious formation and the stock of ideas and images which Christ and the early church used (by selection and transformation) to render his acts intelligible. The New Testament shows the new relationship at work.

Because of their authenticity and their immediacy, both historically and religiously, to the acts, these writings always continue to be directly useful to Christians for edification and for growth in true personal and collective response to God. But for this to happen rightly, it needs to be balanced by their use in a different and more indirect way as a ground for doctrine. Here, we have suggested, they function as specific examples of how the theorem works – examples from a particular period and a particular set of circumstances. New circumstances, new patterns of thought and discourse, produce the need for a continuous stream of new examples, which indeed look back to the first (and subsequent) ones for the guidance they are qualified to give, but do not see them as limiting the area in which the theorem (i.e. the central Christian data) is applicable. In particular, there is no special need for the new doctrinal formulations to use the words and phrases of the old. Indeed we should be on our guard if we find ourselves using them, for they are unlikely to retain their old sense in a changed world.

Christian doctrine is, in sum, the intellectually articulate response of the Christian community to the central data in continually shifting shifting circumstances of culture and thought. The novel feature of our own and recent days has been simply the heightened awareness of these things, bringing with it a new possibility of clarity in our relationship with the formulations of the past, including the New Testament itself. This clarity confers freedom which ought to be received as a blessing.

Catholic teaching, with its emphasis on the role of tradition, has always possessed the seeds of this freedom. It has often used tradition as in effect a burden on the back of scripture, and seen both as vehicles of fixed, oracular authority. By comparison with this, the Reformation plea, continually reiterated, for a return to scripture alone, could only be a liberation. It was intended to be a liberation which would give the word of God free course in the hearts of his people. But, as we are now able to see, there was a need to penetrate further and to make further distinctions, if scripture is not in some ways to obscure him to whom it witnesses.

'Tradition' is a way of referring to what we more generally call the work of the Holy Spirit. The more general term is to be preferred because there is built into it that flexibility and openness to present and future, to the thought and circumstances of the secular world, which we have been commending. Christian doctrine is not a changeless body of truths, formulated and listed for ever, nor is its transmission like the careful handing on of a priceless heirloom which is preserved untouched. Of course in some senses, Christians have long admitted this; they have known that doctrine develops. But that development has been seen as simply the making explicit of what was implicit from the start: in other words, as a self-contained process, taking place in the midst of the world's ordinary history, but detached from it, working by its own inner momentum of grace. Such a view is hardly borne out by the facts. Each growth does not in reality just add enrichment to the already existing stock, as if all took place in the isolation of a cultural incubator and as if there were a settled validity about the fruit of each generation's work. Rather, it is a matter of a series of responses to the divine acts in Christ, responses which always have an experimental nature. They are always attempts to solve a specific problem: how, in the light of *these* circumstances, thinking as we do in the world we live in, do the data appear, and what response do they demand of us? This means that the test of good Christian doctrine lies in its appro-

priateness as response. It also means that no response is the last
word: the terms of the experiment change.

## Notes

1. Ignatius to the Philadelphians 8.2, as translated by Cyril Richardson in *Early Christian Fathers*, Library of Christian Classics I, SCM Press and Westminster Press 1953, p.110.

2. Peter Brown, *Augustine of Hippo*, Faber & Faber and University of California Press 1967, p.253. His chapters 22 and 23 give a most vivid and illuminating account of Augustine's attitude to and use of the Bible.

# 2

# *The Doctrine of the Trinity and the Person of Christ*

The purpose of this article is to examine the connections between various ways of stating some of the fundamental doctrines of the faith, especially as, both in official formularies and in theological discussion, these ways are often not clearly distinguished. Instead, quite inconsistent patterns of thought are freely mixed, so that one finds oneself edged into the hazy world of questions like 'How many apples equal five oranges?' The paper begins by drawing attention to two chief sources of such difficulty; it goes on to explore some of their ramifications in the matters of the Trinity and the person of our Lord; and finally it offers a partial solution.

The first difficulty would be too familiar to mention if it were not still the occasion of so much muddle. It is the failure to separate two ways of using the Bible as a source for Christian doctrine. The first way is to take the Bible simply as a collection of authoritative texts, so that, for example, a doctrine of the Trinity would be sufficiently authorized by the baptismal formula at the end of St Matthew's gospel. Manifestly, no Christians, whatever their profession, have ever used the scriptures in this way *tout court* – or the tale of theological eccentricity would be even odder and longer than it is. The second way of using the Bible as a source of doctrine is to distil from the consensus of scripture a consistent and coherent pattern of teaching, or, to be a little more daring, a dominant pattern; so that, for example, one may hold that nowhere in scripture is the doctrine of the Trinity in its developed form clearly stated, but yet feel impelled to it by the witness of scripture as a whole. This is not what the Bible any-where says, but it *is* what the Bible implies. Now such is the faithfulness to scripture and the intellectual perversity of Christians that we have generally busied ourselves with the second method, while admitting only to the first, quoting texts with a selectivity of whose basis there may be little or no consciousness. For whether it is done with eyes open or closed, this second approach means jettisoning much of what the Bible actually says, and establishing, in the interest of doctrinal consistency, a hierarchy of value among a flat series of texts. Christians have not always found it easy to be clear about the criteria to use in forming that hierarchy.

The second difficulty follows on from the first. It is the difference between formulating doctrine on the direct basis of the facts of revelation in history and on the basis of logical reasoning from those facts. You may believe in the virgin birth of our Lord either because you see it evidenced in scripture and believe it to have happened so, or because you believe that, given certain prior beliefs about God and human nature, it must have occurred in this way or the pattern would not work. But these two approaches may stand in complete independence of each other. One man may believe the fact, yet see no logical connection between it and the rest of his faith. Another will state the faith (i.e., doctrine about God, the person of Christ, and the nature of man) in such a way that the virgin birth has no necessary, or even possible, place in its structure, and, if he is unconvinced by the historical evidence, he will dispense with the fact.

In the case of the doctrine of the Trinity, where we are concerned to make statements about the mode of God's being, the connection between these two ways of arguing is fraught with special hazards. This will come up again in the argument, but it may be mentioned now briefly as a second illustration. Frequently Christians have thought thoughts about the being of God on the basis of what is revealed in history, through scripture. Sometimes before imagination had been quelled by knowledge, they did this with simplicity: as when the three visitors to Abraham in Genesis 18 were seen as a manifestation of God's threefold life. Sometimes in the shape of a providential diagram, as when the scene at our Lord's baptism shows the Three Persons in united but distinguishable action. Sometimes in full rational argument from scripture, as when God is seen to be at work in the world in three separate relationships – as Creator, as incarnate Saviour, and as Sanctifier – and there is seen in this threeness a reflection of the structure of God's inner life. Many indeed would hold that we only know of the Trinity through the revelation in this broad sense, and that any more indirect arguments which might be brought are no more than edifying analogies.

An example of the more indirect kind of argument that arises is this: from the life and death of Jesus we learn that self-giving love is the key characteristic of God. That this is so cannot depend upon the existence of man, a finite being appearing only at a certain point in time, but must be inherent in the divine being. This entails plurality in the Godhead, which might be expressed trinitarianly as Lover, Beloved, and the Love which unites them and in which the one perfectly holds the other. But of course in this argument it is worth noting that it is the plurality that matters more than the threeness, a point to which we shall return. This is not an argument which proceeds by straight lines, so to say, from the activity of God in history, simply pronouncing the fact of threeness and leaving it at that; it is rather an argument which infers the threeness (or plurality) of God from his essential character as made known in Christ. In one sense it could be said to be a legitimate inference, but at a less speculative level it could be said to go beyond the data.

To make the comparison with our first illustration, the doctrine of the virgin birth: on the one hand, just as a man may believe in the virgin birth simply as an act of history without integrating it into the pattern of his belief, so he may believe that God is trinitarian (as an empirically revealed fact) without using it theologically, i.e., without making it signify anything in his theological scheme. He may, for example, just take it as an unfathomable mystery. On the other hand, just as a man may have a scheme of doctrine which includes what, to his mind, the doctrine of the virgin birth is (as he might put it) 'really about', but dispenses with the fact (found to be historically or intellectually implausible); so he may hold to the real intent (as he sees it in the context of his whole pattern of doctrine) of the doctrine of the Trinity, but sit loose to the supposed fact of God's threeness.

This difficulty leads to another closely related to it: the failure to distinguish between speech about God in himself and speech about God as he acts towards us. It *may* be the case that we can have no knowledge of the first and must be content with the second. But supposing, as trinitarian doctrine does suppose, that we can make meaningful statements about God-in-himself, then there is surely no necessarily simple link between the way in which God impinges upon human life, and his own inner being; despite the common assumption that threefold operation on earth discloses threeness in heaven, as directly as if a system of wires, changing from natural to supernatural at the frontier, made the connection.

The difficulties and confusions to which we have referred persist for obvious reasons: the tenacious influence of liturgical and credal formulae, and at a more rarefied level the unfortunate fact that historical theologians and philosophical theologians are not always very literate in one another's fields. Before examining the doctrines of the Trinity and the person of Christ in more detail, we end this discussion of the two difficulties by plumping firmly for one side in each case. As far as the Bible is concerned, we choose the second alternative, and go on to the more drastic step of saying that individual biblical texts have no proper use for us in actually formulating doctrine, except *per accidens* – that is, in cases where a biblical text happens to hit off, illustrate, or roughly correspond to what we wish to say. What they cannot expect is to be guaranteed places in non-biblical frames of discourse. In the case of the second difficulty, we again, at least for the moment, rather crudely choose the second alternative. If it comes to choosing between revealed 'facts' which are theologically useless (in that they do not square with the total pattern), and a total pattern which is consistent and coherent but makes certain so-called facts redundant, we select the second way: though we are fully aware of the simple retort that theological data are in danger of being enslaved to *a priori* schemes. This we accept, while still maintaining our point for the moment, for the sake of the discussion. It entails of course a decision that certain facts are more important than others in forming the total pattern.

Let us now look more closely at the doctrines themselves. We begin with a brief examination of the early centuries in which they found their first formulations, partly because origins always help to explain what follows, partly because confusions such as those we have been discussing there blare forth in pristine cacophony.

Inevitably, any Christian exposition of the divine being begins from either the unity or the plurality. The more orthodox it is, the more it incorporates statements to counterbalance its prevailing tendency, but the chief model will remain. Inevitably too, from earliest times, the readiest analogies for the being of God were drawn from human life: if the tendency is to begin from the divine unity, then the analogy is from the mental workings of the individual; if from the plurality, then from the interrelationship of a group of persons. The status accorded to the analogy varies: for some, it is as closely as possible a picture of reality, the earthly intelligibly mirroring the heavenly; for others it is the haziest approximation to ineffable mystery. In the early years, those whose thought was mainly formed by biblical texts leaned in the first direction; those with more elaborate philosophical training in the second. But all thought of themselves as biblically based, and though this claim was plausibly consistent with either approach to the images, it told more easily in the direction of literalness. Dependence upon scripture by no means settled the issue of preference for divine unity or plurality; biblical texts could be found telling in either sense.

Thus, the Old Testament witness told on the whole and most naturally in favour of the oneness of God as a starting-point. So far as multiplicity was found in relation to God, it was in terms of a wide range of attributes through which he was seen as acting in the world: his word, his wisdom, his breath/spirit, his power, his hand, etc. In the early church, they tended to be seen perhaps rather impersonally, as forces exerted by God, except in so far as in various New Testament writers they had been attached to the person of Christ.

But how exactly was one to know how to distinguish between those Old Testament images which had been given substance and personal content by the coming of Christ and those which had not? The easy answer would lie in an examination of the relevant New Testament texts. But this could not prove satis-factory. Too much had there been said: Jesus was referred to as Son of God, as Word of God, as Wisdom of God; his birth was the result of the action of the Spirit of God, the Power of God, and the Word of God. The only principles to which appeal could be made from this embarrassing richness of biblical texts were the for-mulae already in use in liturgy and Christian instruction, pre-eminently the baptismal formula. And here, enshrined in increasingly revered terms, was threefold structure: Father, Son, and Holy Spirit. As yet, there was no assertion of consubstantial Godhead, but simply (to use the terms we have just had in mind) the singling out of two divine dependencies for special *imprimatur*. That these two terms should be chosen was the result of the accident (theologically speaking) of their collocation in various New Testament texts, such as II Cor. 13.14.

Again theologically speaking, other words might have done duty instead; and if one starts from the fact of the multiplicity of available terms, then it is the formula which serves to call a halt at threefold statement. These terms (though again others might have served) also corresponded to the twin dispensations of divine grace – in the person of Jesus and in the church. This correspondence gives a clear line of rational usefulness for the formula and anchors it in the structure of doctrine. Nevertheless this special exaltation of two of the available terms was something which early Christian thinkers did not always find it easy to explain to themselves, either in terms of logic or when they surveyed the whole range of terms available.[1]

The early church found an intimate link between the accounts given of the being of God and the person of Christ, through the figure of the Logos. This term came to signify (among other things) both the second person of the Trinity and the divine in Christ. But this tie between two doctrines did not necessarily imply any uniformity in what was really in mind in all uses of the word. For some, the Logos remained very much what it was in Old Testament imagery – an attribute of the one God, his powerful agent performing his will in the creation of the world and the direction of affairs. For others, it was the figure of the Wisdom of Solomon and common philosophy, the one mediator between God and this world, spanning the gulf between the transcendent God and the material order. In other words, the Logos could be either impersonal or (at least potentially) personal. Looked at in the first way, the Logos was primarily an impelling force, an outwork of the power of God; looked at in the second way, he easily became a heavenly being, akin to the angelic, only by careful statement raised to oneness with God, either (as in Hebrews 1) by stressing the sonship which differentiated him from those dependencies of God whose status was angelic and no more, or, eventually, by precise metaphysical definition (as at Nicaea). The first way (Logos as divine attribute) constituted no problem for monotheism; the second way (Logos as distinct hypostasis) did. The first way made possible impersonal pluralism in God; the second way was implicitly binitarian from the start. Such was the language. At the level of experience and of formulae, a threefold statement of personal divine reality impressed itself: God was Creator; God was in Christ; God's Spirit empowered Christian life. But how was the experience to be tied to the language?

The lynch-pin was the assertion of the pre-existence of Christ. This belief was fully established in the first decades of the church's existence. In St Paul it is found in I Corinthians, in Philippians, and in Colossians; it is in Hebrews, in St John's gospel, and in the Apocalypse. It was expressed by leaning heavily upon two kinds of Old Testament data which offered themselves to the question. In the first place (as we have seen), Christ was identified with a variety of the attributes of God referred to in the Old Testament (word, wisdom, etc.). But, in the second place, more and more he was *the* Word, the single mediatorial figure between God and the world, the agent of creation (cf. e.g. Ps. 33.6), the spokesman of God through the prophets. So the notion of the personal pre-existence of Christ forced itself upon the church from (*a*) Old Testament texts referring to *the word*, the term unmistakably applied to Jesus in John 1.1-14; (*b*) philosophical notions of a mediatorial principle; (*c*) the speculations of the time about angelic figures, among whom the Logos easily stepped into the position of prince (aided by texts like Isa. 9.5 LXX). All these disparate ideas come together in the key concept of the pre-existence of Christ.

As time went on, the figure of the pre-existent Christ came to play a crucial role in another but related way. He was the link more and more firmly uniting and integrating the account given of the being of God and the account given of the person of Christ. At its simplest, it was a matter of the human Jesus being identified with a heavenly Being who was, with varying degrees of precision, spoken of in divine terms; in more sophisticated words, this heavenly figure was the Second Person of the Trinity, who in Christ took flesh or united to himself human nature. In other words, the Logos performed two parts in the drama, first, as the second element of the divine triad, second, as the divine element in Christ.

Two things deserve notice about this: first, the simple and the sophisticated statements belong to two quite separable and logically unrelated spheres of discourse. The intellectually simple view, whereby the human Jesus is identified with a heavenly Being (angelic in type though formally distinguished from that category) belongs to the sphere of mythology and the cosmic drama. The more sophisticated approach is pure metaphysical philosophy. Yet the distinction between the two was never clearly drawn; elements of both remain intertwined in patristic theological discussion. And secondly: only because these two disparate approaches did find themselves amalgamated was it possible to make an organic tie-up between the two doctrines of the Trinity and the person of Christ. Without the notion of the pre-existent Christ, seen in these ways, the two inquiries could not have been so clearly united.

That marriage, made with more and more precision in the patristic period, has never (so it seems) been seriously interfered with, except at the cost of either a retreat into imprecision of statement or a more or less frank abandonment of traditional orthodox doctrine. For example, those who, over the past century, have been particularly concerned with the historical Jesus in the study of the gospels, or who have emphasized in various ways arguments from religious and moral experience, have been inclined to pay one price or the other. Diffidence in making any statement about the eternal, inner being of God combines with firm concentration on the humanness of Jesus.

Schleiermacher illustrates what we referred to as retreat into imprecision: 'The Redeemer,' he writes, 'is like all men in virtue of the identity of human nature, but is distinguished from them all by the constant potency of his God-consciousness, which was a veritable existence of God in him.'[2] Gospel critics who radically demythologize and assess Jesus in terms of prophetic consciousness (or something like it) illustrate, either explicitly or implicitly, the tendency to abandon all effective statement of orthodox doctrine or to provide no framework within which its statement is possible or relevant. When orthodoxy is maintained, it tends to be still, so far as the Trinity is concerned, in terms of direct inference from the facts and modes of revelation; and, more strikingly for our purposes, it tends to hold on to some version, however disguised, of that bond between the doctrines of the Trinity and of the person of Christ through the pre-existent Logos whose mixed ancestry we have examined.

Professor Hodgson, for example, tries to dispense with it while at the same time firmly retaining it! In his book on *The Doctrine of the Trinity* he first admits that 'in all probability religion will never be able on earth to dispense with this language of pre-existence', then goes on:

> But while religion rightly continues so to think and speak, theology sees clearly the inadequacy both of the language and the thought. Eternity and time are not so related that a life can be thought of as extending for so long in one sphere, then coming down and continuing for some thirty years in the other, and finally returning to go on henceforward in the first. . . . What is sometimes called the doctrine of the pre-existence of Christ is a doctrine which, strictly

speaking, has no meaning unless it means something other than it says. Only in meaning this something other, it means not less than it says, but more. It means that the life about which we read in the Gospels . . . was not a life of which the whole story was told between the earthly birth and death, as it is with each of us. It expresses the recognition that it was the earthly life of One who was somehow essentially different from every one of us. How great that difference was the Christian Church came clearly to state when at Nicaea the words 'of one substance with the Father' were written into the Creed . . . [This statement] substituted . . . a timeless truth for the recitation of an impossible bit of history. Instead of trying to extend the true history fore and aft into eternity, it directed attention to the essential qualitative difference between one historic Figure and all others.[3]

There are more difficulties in this than we can look at, but chiefly it seems to applaud a statement which, with whatever changes in the idiom, is not substantially different from the older dramatic language which it seeks to replace. However much more sophisticated the language of Nicaea, it in no way throws over or denies (or even explicitly questions) the older and simpler approach. It is very doubtful whether the fathers of AD 325 would have welcomed praise for substituting 'a timeless truth' (whatever that may be!) for 'an impossible bit of history'. Further, Professor Hodgson's own account of the 'something other' speaks of *a* life shared by the pre-existent and historical Christ and refers to him as a 'One' – terms of personal identity not essentially removed from the older, less abstract imagery.

Earlier, we distinguished, by way of illustrating two different approaches to the forming of Christian doctrine, two ways of coming to the doctrine of the Trinity. We shall now examine them in more detail. The first way, of which we disapproved, reads off the heavenly from the earthly. According to this way, God appears to us in three distinct relationships (of creation, redemption, and sanctification) and this means that God is threefold personal existence. In fact, it entails merely the lesser mystery of divine versatility.

The second way (that of reasoning on the basis of the revealed nature of God) provides other supports for the doctrine of the Trinity which are logically quite independent of the first way. We give two examples. First, in his mental workings, man can be seen to be an instance of personal multiplicity in unity – he unites in himself, for example, memory, understanding, and will. But man is made in the divine image; and so multiplicity in unity can also be posited as true of God, whom man reflects. This can be used merely as a providential analogy for trinitarian doctrine, while the *ground* for that doctrine is still found in the facts of revelation. But it can instead be more firmly integrated into the doctrinal pattern, as our statement of it suggests. We expounded our second example earlier. In Christ, God is revealed as love, and this fact argues for mutuality in the divine being. These two lines of argument, the one from man as the summit of creation, the other from what Christ revealed to be the truth about God, are both logically independent of the line which simply reads off the being of God from the triple mode of divine action in the world. We now place this last line of argument firmly in the background and consider further the other two.

First, it is worth noting that while the first (that from the human mind) leads to an emphasis on divine unity, for the unity of man is more striking than the multiplicity of his mental activities, the second leads to stress on plurality, for love requires at least two parties. In that sense the two lines of thought are complementary.

Secondly, neither of them involves the notion of the pre-existence of Christ, nor at all easily accommodates it. The second argument in particular clearly shifts the imagery away from such a possibility. If Christ discloses the fact of mutuality in the being of God by the character of his life and death, this neither demands nor easily allows that he be seen as the Second Person of the Trinity come to earth. In the terms of this argument, Christ, by his self-giving to God and man, shows love to be the key characteristic of God: it is a quite distinct question to see what that love implies for the inner being of God.

Thirdly, neither of these arguments really involves trinity. The first admits multiplicity, the second runs well on duality. On either of these lines of argument, it appears that while plurality *can* be said to be true of God, threeness is of no particular help or importance. In fact, the least important fact about the Trinity turns out to be its threeness!

These two arguments eliminate the pre-existence of Christ. What then are we to say of it? Let us try saying that it is simply part of the mythological furniture of the first century, which was given a firm niche in Christian formulation through (*a*) the fact that it accorded so well with numerous scriptural texts, in Old and New Testaments, wherein the church sought to find primary authority; (*b*) the fact that it was congenial to contemporary religious speculation and to contemporary philosophy, then coming more and more closely together. It began (for example, in Phil. 2.6-11) as frankly mythological, in the sense of giving a description of supernatural realities as wholly continuous with the observable world. But later, when it received metaphysical statement, it could never abandon its mythological side, simply because it was, after all, a statement about the previous life of one who had actually lived in the world and was known from the pages of the gospels. It could never become pure philosophy.

But if this link between the doctrine of the Trinity and the doctrine of the person of Christ is removed, does any link remain? Not in what might be called an organic sense: that is, not in the sense that the pre-existent Christ in classical statement provided it. These two doctrines should be formulated separately, with the aid of quite distinct images and models of discourse.

Normally, when the liaison between them has been broken, it has been, as we have suggested, at the price of despair about saying anything at all concerning God's inner being, and often at the cost of any effective statement of Christ's divinity. No such disastrous and radical results are necessary. The separation of the two doctrines is necessary and beneficial for the invigoration of both. To take first the doctrine of the Trinity: to be theologically and religiously useful, this doctrine (like any other) must be shown to be related integrally to the action of Christ, to human life, and to Christian life. The mere assertion that God had revealed himself in threefold relationship with us never acted in this way. It found illuminating analogies in human life; it provided a Baedeker to that life of God into which we are baptized; it gave an interesting and edifying fact; but it has never been theologically or religiously *useful*. For religious usefulness in particular, Christians have always had recourse to the other two lines of argument to which we have referred. In other words, for a doctrine of God ultimately to be useful to my soul, if I am to learn what it is to be a partaker of the divine nature (and whatever is included in that kind of expression of Christian status), it must be a statement that is really about the inner being of God, and not merely his activity in history. It *is* religiously and theologically useful to me in this sense to know that God is the fount and centre of love, that relationships fragmented here are perfected in the divine life. Of this the doctrine of the Trinity (though the number is immaterial) is the assertion. To know that threefold operation mirrors threefold being is not useful in this sense.

The doctrine of the person of Christ similarly benefits from the severance of the cord which has traditionally bound it to the doctrine of the Trinity. As long as Christ is seen as the incarnate Second Person of the Trinity, whatever terminology is used, and however one tries to distinguish the metaphysical level of statement from the physical, it is impossible fully to lay the ghost of mythology. It is also well-nigh impossible to give a satisfactory account of the humanity of Jesus without compromising the oneness of his person, or perhaps even to give an account of his full humanity at all. This is not the place for technicalities, but certainly within the terms of patristic theology, the Chalcedonian Definition achieves a settlement of the most fragile satisfactoriness, threatening to dissolve at the merest touch. Certainly too the kenotic theories of Gore and others, attempting to take serious account of Christ's human limitations in respect of knowledge, present an incredible mechanism, a hardly imaginable identity between the pre-existent and incarnate Christ.

Any modern statement of the doctrine must start from the datum of the humanity of Jesus. The danger is that, for reasons of modern prejudice or lack of a congenial language, it will also stop there, seeing Jesus as the 'man for others', or the high-water mark of religious genius. The problem is to give a satisfactory account of his divinity which (a) does not impair his humanity; (b) is not philosophically or psychologically unconvincing and unhelpful (as the traditional language about divine and human natures is to all but a few); (c) makes clear the uniqueness of Jesus and does not reduce him to one of a class, even if the highest member of the class, of divinely inspired persons. Freed from the need to dovetail our statement with trinitarian doctrine, that is, no longer being compelled to see him as what amounts to the human manifestation of the Second Person of the Trinity (whatever idiom may be employed), we are in a position to start with a cleaner sheet than would otherwise be possible. We can look at christology in itself and frame our model as best suits the case, without reference to patterns helpful and appropriate in framing trinitarian doctrine.

Let us turn to the notion of salvation-history as a starting-point. Jesus is man, open, like all men, to many kinds of inquiry and definition. If we ask about him the historian's questions, we find in him only the same sort of uniqueness as can be found in any of us. Even when he is explained in terms of categories such as 'founder of a religion' or 'miracle-worker', there are others alongside him. 'If I by Beelzebub cast out devils, by whom do your sons cast them out?' He appears significantly unique only if we ask the question about his role in the divine work in history, in relation to the role of the rest of us in the same work. We can put it thus: the process of God's self-disclosure which is at work in the religious history of Israel and in his gracious activity in humanity as a whole came to a personal and individual consummation in Jesus; in him the self-disclosure of God is concentrated, fulfilled, completely personalized, by contrast with other impersonal, partial expressions of divine being and will.

In terms of function performed, God is active wholly in each of us for bringing us to perfect relationship with himself, and what we do by way of co-operation is all in response to him. God is active in Jesus, by contrast, to make himself clear and to elicit that response from us. This unique function which it is his to perform in the setting of human history in no way conflicts with his humanity: any more than the different function which God performs in us casts doubt upon the genuineness of our humanity. The problem of the divinity of Christ is no different from the problem of grace in us, except for the historical setting and role. Christ is no automaton in fulfilling his historical role, any more than we are when we fit into a niche largely determined by our family, our society, and our culture. Jesus freely gives himself to the performance of the role into which he enters. So far as the self-giving is concerned, he is comparable with any great saint, but in the role and function for which he gives himself he is utterly unique. By fitting into the role as hand into glove, his action is not simply superbly God-directed human action, but divine action – and in this sense (though the language is almost inevitably bound up with the concepts we wish to avoid), Jesus is divine.

This is not then the action of the Second Person of the Trinity (even with customary safeguards about the whole Godhead being present in the activity of each Person): it is the action of God, as he is in himself, a God, that is, characterized by the mutuality of love, acting as he can only act when doing it through a human person who is wholly open to him and is formed for this very role. In certain respects, he acts in Christ exactly as in each of us, but the role and function in the setting of history are unique. Austin Farrer makes the point thus:

> In the common case of a good human life, humanity supplies the pattern, God the grace. In Jesus, divine redemptive action supplies the

pattern and manhood the medium or instrument. A good man helped by grace may do human things divinely; Christ did divine things humanly.[4]

The old patristic doctrine endeavoured to show that God was wholly present in Christ without remainder: he was personally God. But this cannot be so in every sense. As an attempt to say that in him man was encountering no less than God, it was right and true, and we have tried to outline a position which says nothing other than this. As an attempt to say that in existing in the human mode, God suffered no limitation of any kind, it said more than was either possible or necessary. More than was possible, because it can hardly be formulated without doing violence to our Lord's humanity. More than was necessary, because in many respects, Christ's limitations (e.g. his ignorance of Swahili or nuclear physics) are without relevance to his role. Clearly in the days of his flesh he could as an individual do only what is possible within the limits of individual existence. Thus, as revealing God to be characterized in his rule of all things by love and perfect self-giving, he could indeed act with supreme generosity, even to the cross. He could show and work out perfect relationship with God, and this was an unveiling of the divine life; but he could not exhibit the perfection of self-giving in all the varied relationships which constitute life in society. Yet this is something equally necessary for planting charity among us and for working out reconciled human life in the world. It is the church's role from the start to perform this function, and it is in this sense that the church can be said to extend the incarnation. In this area we are meeting a different function for God's action, a role related to that of Christ but also distinct from it.

We have tried to see what happens when the imagery and language binding together the two doctrines of the Trinity and the person of Christ are sundered. The bond is a hangover from mythology into Christian metaphysics. In certain ways it has caused chronic, yet unnecessary, difficulties for Christian theology. At root, behind the rather hard and fast metaphysical structure of the early centuries, lies the Bible with its great variety of imagery and terminology for God's being and activity. At certain points, the way these terms take their place in doctrinal formulation seems to a considerable degree to be fortuitous theologically. The one is taken and the other left.

Moreover there seem to be two quite unrelated ways of applying the biblical revelation to the doctrine of God. We do not mean the important but relatively simple matter of seeing behind the texts to the whole drift of the Bible's teaching, which, especially in the light of historical criticism, certainly eliminates many errors and pseudo-problems. We refer rather to the distinction between on the one hand seeing threefold being in God as revealed in three modes of divine activity on earth and arguing from the second to the first, and on the other inferring the nature of God from the make-up of man, made in his image, and above all from the character, acts and teaching of Christ. The latter seems in many ways to be preferable, and leads to the conclusion that mutuality rather than threeness is what really matters about God. This approach enables the severance of the two doctrines to be carried out, opening up a quite distinct line of argument for formulating our belief in the divinity of Christ, one related to his unique function in the history of salvation.

## Notes

1. See e.g. Tertullian, *Adversus Praxean* 26 (ed. E. Evans, SPCK and Macmillan, New York, 1948, p.170).

2. Friedrich Schleiermacher, *The Christian Faith*, ed. H. R. Mackintosh and J. S. Stewart, T. & T. Clark and Scribner's 1928, p.385.

3. Leonard Hodgson, *The Doctrine of the Trinity*, Nisbet 1943, Scribner's 1944, pp.65f.

4. Austin Farrer, *Saving Belief,* Hodder & Stoughton 1964, Morehouse-Barlow 1965, p.75.

# 3

## *The Place of Jesus*

God broods over the New Testament, but Jesus fills the foreground. If we transfer its reference from the New Testament to the world, that sentence could almost be a summary of the prologue of the Fourth Gospel. But whatever the reference, does it not present us with a theological picture whose measure we are reluctant to take? The pattern it reflects is surely bound to be problematic for us, in two respects.

First, there is the question of the proper direction of thrust in expounding the Christian faith in our society. Should we start with God or with Jesus? Some of those who choose the latter do so because they are sceptical of God's existence, at least in the traditional senses, but find in Jesus the focus of faith, devotion and inspiration. More do so because they share the New Testament's perspective and, taking God without question, let Jesus fill the foreground of their attention and discourse. Sometimes of course the doctrinal backing is traditional and orthodox, that is, it is thoroughly theistic, and the reason for what may appear an over-emphasis on Jesus is mainly tactical: here is the most attractive and convenient point of entry to a faith which can be expounded later in more systematic fashion. Sometimes, however, the effect is *as if* God did not exist, and the links with traditional Christianity become tenuous. There is then at least a possibility of distortion or imbalance when, in presenting the Christian faith in our society, we follow the recipe stated in our opening sentence, letting Jesus fill the foreground and leaving God, implicitly and at least in certain respects, in the background.

It will of course be replied that for a Christian, to speak of Jesus is to speak of God, to expound christology is to expound theism. But even the most devoted adherent of Nicene orthodoxy will admit a certain priority to the question of God over the question of Jesus, will see the latter in the setting of the former, and will recognize the dangers of anything that looks at all like a foot-loose 'Christ-religion'.

Unless we are to adopt a most extreme doctrine of development or an extreme degree of demythologizing (as for example Alistair Kee in *The Way of Transcendence*[1]), any exposition of what can purport to be New Testament faith must penetrate behind the appearances and place God before Jesus. The situation in which that exposition now takes place fortifies this policy. For while the New Testament was written in a world where belief in the divine was normal and lively, our society presents a quite different face; and where there is any serious enquiry into religious questions it is likely to be at the level of wondering whether there is anything at all in 'the divine dimension'. Tactically or emotionally prior in certain circumstances perhaps, the place of Jesus is logically secondary; it is also secondary from the point of view of the demands of our current religious situation. God needs to have a more active role in our theological picture than to brood over it.

If we now take the matter away from apologetic, we encounter a theological problem which stands in its own right. *God broods over the New Testament, but Jesus fills the foreground.* Does the New Testament give to us, as we read it today, a fair impression of the shape of the theology which its writers held? And even if it does, were they possibly carried away, beyond what could properly be affirmed, by the novelty and force of their experience of Jesus? For reasons which are not wholly theological, does the New Testament give an exaggerated place to Jesus, which needs to be corrected not only because of certain apologetic needs but at the level of theology itself?

The questions are posed from the point of view of the modern reader looking back at the New Testament. But another aspect of the matter is this: did the patristic builders of classical Christian doctrine, in taking New Testament texts at their face value without attempting to penetrate into their pedigree or the living circumstances of the first century, find themselves impelled into a view of Jesus which not only failed to grasp the 'real shape' of the New Testament writers' theology but also accorded him a place unwarranted by a 'proper' understanding of those documents? This question goes beyond our present scope. It is much more complex because it involves the whole question of the conditions under which concepts may be re-expressed in fresh philosophical contexts. But in so far as the patristic formulations retain a place in church language, the question imposes itself. We turn, however, to the New Testament.

To sharpen our focus, let us put up a hypothesis which may be fit only to go the way of many predecessors; and then let us unravel a story which expounds it.

The hypothesis is this: that the first Christians found their attitude on all fundamental questions so transformed as a result of Jesus that they could only speak of him in language which was hyperbolic rather than sober, evaluative rather than factual, and riotously diverse rather than carefully consistent. This is the first step in a particular kind of christology. This christology rests on certain convictions: that experience of Jesus, direct or indirect, is at the heart of the matter; that the words in which the experience was expressed must, for their proper understanding, be traced to their roots in that experience; and that these words (e.g. the titles of Jesus) are attempts to objectify that experience, to transfer it from the heart of the believer and place it 'out there' in the world of external 'facts'.

Still further back lies this belief which must be left for the moment in the form of assertion: that doctrinally speaking christology is, in the New Testament, despite all appearances, wholly secondary. It is a disguised way of speaking about God. This is true not in the sense that the early Christians did not really believe they were making statements about Jesus, but in the sense that the experience those statements reflect was in fact concerned primarily and ultimately with God. The attitudes which were transformed were, at the deepest level, attitudes to God, then, secondarily and dependently, attitudes to the world, to oneself, to human relationships and society, and indeed to Jesus himself.

There is of course a half-concealed empiricism in all this which had better come into the open. Theology is subjective human language, it is not objectively descriptive language about God. It suffers (or benefits!) therefore, like all other language, especially that which goes beyond the most direct account of sense-data, from fragility and mobility. While it often represents a consensus of agreement (and therefore is not subjective in the purely individual sense), it is nevertheless deceptive when it appears to be giving a 'solid' account of God. It is not merely that it is analogical (that when God is described as 'loving' or addressed as 'father', our use of these terms in ordinary life applies only so far and in certain respects); it is also that the words themselves shift in meaning from one speaker or culture to another (my father colours my use of the word as your father colours yours, and a thirteenth-century Polish father is not wholly like a twentieth-century American one). Shifts may be small, but they are constant, and variety of experience lies behind them.

While it is controlled by formulation and tradition (working at least implicitly on a more optimistic view of the solidity of language), talk about God is peculiarly open to this fragility and mobility, for its subject is not exposed to sight or touch. In this sense he is at the mercy of the human imagination. At the same time theological language is peculiarly prone to arouse claims for its solidity. The investment of allegiance and devotion in God transfers itself, inevitably, it appears, to language about him: if he is rock-like and eternal, so are the propositions concerning him. In an area where mobility of language is high, willingness to recognize it is low.

We wish to give that mobility full recognition. We wish also to give full value to the change that comes over language when it moves from the factual to the evaluative. It becomes less controllable, more mobile. It becomes more a matter of impression and opinion. It becomes more expressive of shallowness or depth of feeling and conviction. All language about God, in the end, bears this character, and the closer it is to roots in experience and the further away from purely intellectual formulation, the more this is so.

This is no comment on the question of the 'truth' or 'falsity' of the language in question. It is comment on the conditions under which language concerning God can point to truth: on its limitations and its possibilities. For the mobility and fragility of language are not matters for regret or for 'getting round'. They alone make it possible for the language to reflect rather than suppress the ever-changing variety of experience. They are the conditions by which spontaneity and immediacy can play a part in religious discourse and by which it can respond to developments in other spheres of thought.

The period of the early church was one in which these qualities were abundantly present. It is therefore not surprising that, according to our hypothesis, the language was hyperbolic rather than sober, evaluative rather than factual, and riotously diverse rather than carefully consistent. And the language of christology was disguised language about God because it reflected transformed attitudes to God. How does this work?

We do not know the precise nature of Jesus' personality and if we met him we should differ about it; nor do we know the exact content of his message. However, we do know a considerable amount about the effects of both his teaching and his career. It may not be possible to argue very accurately from the observable effects to a description of the causes, that is to a description of Jesus' person and teaching. But certain probabilities will emerge and we shall at least feel confident in asserting the intensity of his influence in certain directions. Nevertheless the nature of the experience to which the historical Jesus gave rise (indirectly in all cases that are observable to us, but in some ways all the more impressive for that) is our firm starting-point. It is the beginning of Christian theology.

Experience gives rise to formulation, and, especially when words are being given new applications, is very close to it. In such cases, the words explode into existence from the interior force of the experience: so a poet may coin words only intelligible to those able to some degree to share his mind, and the man seized by religious ecstasy may utter sounds which strike others as pure nonsense. The words are selected not for their coherence with each other, but for their appropriateness as expressions of some aspect of the experience. The more vivid the experience, the more likely it is that the words chosen will have an impressionistic quality. Not all sides of their existing sense will necessarily apply; rather they will catch, in some striking way and perhaps with only one facet of their significance, the sense of the experience. This facet may be so isolated and exaggerated that, effectively, the word receives a new meaning – merits a new entry in the dictionary.

The process can be most neatly demonstrated with regard to some of the titles of Jesus. For this purpose it does not matter whether they were claimed by Jesus himself or accorded to him by early Christians. In the former case, they arose from Jesus' own understanding of his role or, in our terms, from his own 'experience of himself'. It is easier, however, if we consider them as they were used by his followers. Then we can see how they arose from attitudes transformed as a result of Jesus. Moreover we can see something of the process at work in the pages of the New Testament.

Let us examine cases. First, one which does not have the complication of having led to later dogmatic formulation. It retains therefore for us something of the informal character which it has in the New Testament. Paul sees Jesus as parallel to Adam – a second Adam, reproducing his role as head and fount of the race but reversing his dreadful inheritance (Rom. 5.12ff.; I Cor. 15.21f., 45ff.). The relatively informal character of this language means that we scarcely think of 'last Adam' (I Cor. 15.45) as a *title* for Jesus or as an 'objective' description. We do not immediately range it with Messiah, Son of God, or Son of man. We might instead speak of it as an image, or, more technically, a piece of typology.

But prior to that, it is the expression of a certain quality of conviction about Jesus, and, more deeply, the expression of experience brought about by him. Can we be precise about the character of that experience? It found appropriate expression in language about Adam, the father of the race. It must therefore have represented experience which we might express, in rather pretentious jargon, as 'a rejuvenation of a sense of being human'. That is, the experience was individual, but it related to one's awareness of solidarity with one's fellows. We may suppose that for Paul the experience at this level was both profound and crucial: how else may we explain his vital (and original?) sense of the universality of Christ's significance and of the abolition of the distinction of value between Gentile and Jew?

Now it is usual to suppose that Paul's language concerning Adam and Christ arose from reflection upon scripture and from quasi-dogmatic convictions about its fulfilment. But on any showing Paul is highly selective in his use of the Old Testament, and we have to enquire what led to the selection he made. The answer lies, we suggest, at least with regard to this example, in an experience, brought about as a result of Jesus and giving rise to a conviction about man's new potentialities.

If we go on to ask how Jesus brought about such an experience, so giving rise to such a conviction, we are immediately on uncertain ground. Was it an overwhelming sense of the simplicity and directness of Jesus' teaching about God which evoked the feeling that this was of universal human import? Or was it derived from other features of the experience of which he was the cause? Thus: as a result of him, there was a sense of forgiveness and release so profound that it could not but be available equally to all men. Was it, that is, Jesus' effect upon his followers' sense of their relationship with God rather than their apprehension of God that spread into a sense of its universality? The route by which Jesus impelled Paul to the conviction that he could be described as (or even was) the last Adam is not clear to us – Paul does not show his working and was quite probably unaware of it. What we can say is that as a result of Jesus (whether his teaching or his whole career or some elements within it), Paul's sense of what it meant to belong to the human race was so transformed that this startling language arose as alone adequate to the need.

Other titles given to Jesus function by comparable but quite distinct lines of working. For example, he is God's creative and pre-existent Word (John 1.1-14; I Cor. 8.6; Heb. 1.3). In this case, a factor absent from our previous case enters the discussion. That Jesus was the Word was to become a matter not merely of isolable or occasional scriptural exegesis but of coherent dogmatic statement. Moreover it led to convictions about his biography: he had existed from all eternity. To all appearances, that is, it added to the stock of facts about him.

But what could possibly lead to the according of such a status and the attribution of such a 'fact' to a man of flesh and blood? The usual answer of historical criticism is familiar: whatever its later development in a Greek milieu, the idea has its roots in Judaism, and on that basis is perfectly explicable. The Jews were accustomed to attribute pre-existence to those features of their religion to which they gave special value as mediators of the knowledge and activity of God, supremely but not exclusively the law. This tendency to hypostatize or make 'solid' realities in the divine sphere out of earthly concepts (e.g. wisdom) or religiously valuable objects (e.g. the law) was of long standing in Judaism and was not surprisingly transferred to Jesus by Jewish Christians, who ascribed to him the supreme religious value which they had formerly discerned elsewhere. Indeed, they saw him as unique in this respect, and so in the New Testament writings he steps into the place of all the great mediators of Judaism – God's wisdom, his word, the law, the temple. Not all writers worked this out over the same range of ideas and some never took the step of putting Jesus into the place of any of the entities regarded by Jews as pre-existent. So while the gospel of John attributes pre-existence to him (as it works with the idea of the Word), neither Matthew nor Luke has any clear trace of it.[2]

So the answer runs, and it is of course accurate – as far as it goes. But it scarcely explores to the full how there came to be ascribed to Jesus a title which signified not only pre-existence but also creativity. Was it just a matter of reflecting a sense of his supreme significance? The question remains: what could possibly lead to the according of such a role, that of God's agent in creation, to a man?

The Johannine tradition reached the point of ascribing it to Jesus' own claim for himself (8.58; 12.41): he himself was the source of this belief. But even if we were to accept these sayings as authentic and even if we were to see them in the setting of classical Chalcedonian teaching, we are still concerned to ask how a human self-consciousness could arrive at such a formulation of its understanding of itself.

If instead we adopt the assumption that the sayings are not authentic and that we cannot look to Jesus as the source of this belief, we turn instead to Christian experience. Taking the same path of argument as in our earlier example, must we not say that the understanding of Jesus as the pre-existent agent in creation was rooted in an experience, as a result of him, of freshness in relation to *everything*? The first Christians (we may express it thus) looked out on a new world, a universe transfigured. We can even lay our hands on an early stage in the process: 'When anyone is united to Christ, there is a new world; the old order has gone, and a new order has already begun' (II Cor. 5.17 NEB). Of course this is rooted in current eschatological hope: but the question is, what brought that hope into play in this particular form? To answer that we must penetrate deeper than the examination of the Jewish background to Paul's ideas and ask about the experience which led him to draw upon certain areas of language and imagery rather than others.

Two questions and one conclusion follow. We raise the questions rather than answer them.

First, how did Jesus give rise to an experience of such wide and deep ramifications? We cannot tell how far it was the effect of his teaching, how far the impact of his whole career, how far the force of his person expressed first by direct contact and then by reputation.

Second, how far was it a genuinely theological experience and how far emotional? That is, were the early Christians who reacted thus to Jesus in any way justified in drawing theological inferences from their experience, or should they have stopped at the simple conclusion: 'Jesus is wonderful. He makes the world feel different to me.' Was that what they *really* meant, or was there sense in moving on from that expression of *feeling* to statements about the true nature of the world's relationship with God and Jesus' crucial role in that relationship?

Again, the evidence is not wholly lacking. The experience was not one of enthusiasm merely for Jesus' person, still less one of undirected euphoria, but seems to have *involved* a renewed apprehension of the world's nature and destiny. So Paul saw the natural order itself as destined for salvation (Rom. 8.19ff.).

It is arguable of course that Paul arrived at this doctrine by a process of argument, or rather that it was part and parcel of his eschatological beliefs. But there was nothing in these beliefs to compel him to see Jesus, even if he was the central actor in the eschatological drama, as the pre-existent agent of creation. At this early stage, when there was still a struggle to arrive at appropriate words, the experience is dominant. The universe had been made through Jesus at the start (I Cor. 8.6) because for Paul it had been remade through Jesus in his own unmistakable experience.

A parallel will shed some light. Edwin Muir's poem 'The Trans-figuration'[3] and G. M. Hopkins's 'The world is charged with the grandeur of God'[4] express a comparable vision of the world's true nature. If the vision were to be translated into a message, it would be that we must look beneath the surface of things if we would see their real value and that the world in all its parts is the beloved creation of the living God. We must cast off our customary dullness and flatness of vision, for the world is full of beauty, vitality and hope. The sense of near ecstasy which the poems reflect extends to and is of a piece with a genuine apprehension of the world as related to God which is capable of propositional statement.

So for the early Christians, the experience of Jesus seems to have carried with it a transformed attitude to the world. This meant not so much new beliefs about it as an intensified and heightened awareness of its status as the creature of God. And deeper still and prior to it lay a renewed awareness of God himself. That, we may suppose, was the main thrust of Jesus' impact upon his followers.

The conclusion is this: that the description of Jesus as the pre-existent and creative Word was a projection into 'objective' language, by a process wholly intelligible on the Jewish back-ground, of a transformed awareness of the world, which was in turn derived from the understanding of God and the form of relationship with him which Jesus had so compellingly con-veyed.

The remaining point of obscurity is the nature of the force

which clearly came from Jesus to produce effects so deep and comprehensive in the attitudes of his first adherents. The obscurity has two dimensions. There is the historical problem, for the solution of which the evidence is simply insufficient. And there is the question of faith involving the theological problem concerning God's action here as anywhere. It is important to identify the point of obscurity as exactly as possible, or else we shall see mystery where there is only muddle.

The other titles of Jesus, and indeed more complex statements about him, are equally open to treatment along these lines.[5] We have chosen for detailed examination two claims made for him which from the point of view of plain statement seem peculiarly extravagant. Other titles are often taken to be in some sense more 'literal' or 'objective': Jesus *was* Son of God or Son of man, Jesus *is* Lord. The understanding of all these titles is complicated at the purely historical level by the likelihood that they had meant a number of different things by the time they reached written expression in the New Testament. But each of them reflects a certain facet of experience of Jesus leading to a particular strand of conviction. The title is earthed in the experience; whether the experience be one of a new immediacy of relationship with God, as a result of Jesus (so Jesus is Son of God), or one of absolute confidence in God for the future (so Jesus is the Son of man of apocalyptic hope).

Messiah, which we are often inclined to see as the simplest title of all, is in some ways the most surprising. It must have burst from the experience with the peculiar power of paradox. For Jesus betrayed few of the stock messianic characteristics: military leadership, this-worldly rule and victory, and fervent patriotism. How then did the title emerge? It must have sprung from an overwhelming sense that he was God's agent for the satisfying of his people's deepest needs; and behind that from an experience, occasioned by him, of certainty that God's cause, now widened in scope, was moving towards its triumphant vindication.

This approach to the teaching of the New Testament about Jesus yields a simple, even at first sight platitudinous result. People turned to Christianity because they experienced, as a result of Jesus, a transformation of their attitudes to God and to everything. This is a statement of plain history. Put as a christological proposition, it goes: Jesus is the one who, as a matter of fact, produced this transformation of attitudes to God and to everything. Or in theistic terms: God, and everything as depending upon him, is best understood in the manner which results from the impulse derived from Jesus.

An interesting line of enquiry would be: in what sense, if any, is such a set of statements a fair re-expression, in fairly severely empirical terms, of Nicene orthodoxy, whose philosophical assumptions are so different and whose claims appear at first sight so much higher? Meanwhile, our statements can claim certain advantages. First, they place the point of Christian distinctiveness and so decision where it ought to be placed: do you believe in God in the manner which results from the impulse derived from Jesus? That is, theism is the beginning and end of the matter. Second, it takes seriously the necessarily negative nature of discourse about the 'inner workings' of God. We can make no strictly descriptive statements about the divine – but we are continually reluctant to accept the fact! We can speak only of our experience of him and we can *believe* that the experience is not misleading. A Christian is one who finds the source of that experience (by whatever long route it came to him) in Jesus, and he is a Christian because he judges that experience to be uniquely illuminating and fundamentally significant.

Our approach does not only claim advantages, it also points a finger of warning.

We have held that the christological statements of the New Testament are 'projections' in ostensibly descriptive and literal language of experience concerning God and the world to which Jesus gave rise or to which he at least gave decisively new shape. We have suggested that the experience and the statements are utterly bound together: the latter spring straight out of the former. We have suggested too that the experience is the point of primary interest and importance, theologically and religiously, and that it is in principle capable of quite different verbal expression. Moreover, its bearing is clarified if it does receive a variety of verbal expression, for it can then be shown to be concerned above all with a strong and sharp awareness of God and of relationship with him: such awareness is bound to result in constantly fresh verbal formulation. We judge too that this approach not only uncovers the workings of the New Testament propositions about Jesus but also makes possible the use in speech about him of our present, ordinary language, by relating all formulations to the experience, which is nearer the centre. In the experience the lines converge more clearly than in the language. So this method removes certain strains – or rather places the strain where it ought to be, in the issue of theistic faith.

It follows that the whole matter is put in jeopardy when the statements which in New Testament days fittingly expressed Christian experience (but have now become technical terms and no longer current speech) are divorced from it, and used by those who, whatever their stated beliefs, do not share it. Thus, when Jesus is referred to as the Word, the agent in creation, simply as a description of his place in the divine sphere, and there is no longer any sense of a world transformed; or when Jesus is called Son of man, but his followers no longer have any vivid assurance or hope; or when he is called Son of God, but Christians lack any strong sense of God's immediacy; then the fatal divorce has taken place and the structure of the earliest Christian theologies observable in the New Testament has begun to collapse. Over large tracts of Christian history and life the divorce between experience and statement has been endemic and Christians have lived in 'the old world' on a theistic belief which includes a seat for Jesus in the heavenly places. The framing of creeds and articles as tests of belief has, whatever its merits, been the danger signal that the divorce is on the way, for then the literally descriptive element is likely to be winning independent life.

A final remark. While many Christians still hold to the New Testament in an uncritical way which does little credit to belief in a living Creator God, others have virtually abandoned it as an effective guide, and the question of the use of the Bible imposes itself on the church.

One important and necessary use of the New Testament, and particularly its earlier writings produced when the struggle for formulation was still visibly in progress, is to show both that experience is properly anterior to statement and that the two must be indissoluble if distinctively Christian faith is to persist. If the experience is authentic and valid, the statement may be trusted to find its own proper form. Renewal must still find its source in the New Testament. The common error is to think that it should stop there.

## Notes

1. Alistair Kee, *The Way of Transcendence*, Penguin 1971.
2. But see R. G. Hamerton-Kelly, *Pre-existence, Wisdom, and the Son of Man*, Cambridge University Press 1973, ch. 2.

3. Edwin Muir, *Collected Poems*, Faber & Faber 1960, p.198.

4. G. Manley Hopkins, *Poems*, Oxford University Press 1948, p.70.

5. For an examination of the language of atonement in the New Testament from this standpoint, see John Knox, *The Death of Christ*, Abingdon Press 1958, Collins 1959, pp.146ff.

# 4

## *The Idea of the Church*

The disparity between the church's profession and the facts of its life has always been a theoretical as well as a practical problem in one form or another, whether recognized or not. Attempts to relieve it, or even to solve it, may be made at a number of levels. The historian will point to the evidence: yes, it is true that the church's performance has constantly failed to match its ideals, but there is also much to be said on the other side. Sin is balanced by sanctity, and the fair-minded observer will allow both to form his judgment.

More theologically, distinctions may be drawn within the historical church between the outward husk of formal Christians whose heart is not with the Lord, whatever their verbal confession and observance, and the kernel of true believers, discernible, perhaps, only to the eye of God, but nevertheless the carriers of the gospel from one age to another. Whether this inner core of witness is identified with particular organs of the church (e.g. religious orders) or with independent sects or with a certain quality of allegiance, the principle is the same. Wheat and tares co-exist in the mixed body; while there may be guesses about the identity of each, it is not essential that they should be clearly known.

It is possible to be more abstract and to distinguish not two kinds of persons but two aspects of the same persons. The same group of people (that is, the church) may be at one and the same time both sinners and the immaculate body of Christ. Fallible and peccable outwardly, they may in their inward reality as the instrument of God's purposes be both sinless and infallible. Christians – all Christians – may err, the church cannot. It is a position which demands a most tenacious hold on a sort of dogmatic Platonism, and few are those who can hold to it rigorously while they contemplate the facts of church life past and present. So radical a cleavage between the observable reality and the idea of the church strains credulity – or faith – to breaking-point; even the determined philosopher will look for the facts to reflect rather than deny the truth which he believes to lie concealed at the heart of things. And if for 'the heart of things' we substitute, more Christianly, 'the mind of God', then the difficulty is, if anything, intensified; for how can we believe that the intelligence behind and in all things hoodwinks himself, or is so determinedly teleogical, as this formulation so strongly suggests?

All in all, this traditional 'solution' commends itself less and less to Christian opinion. Not only does it strain credulity in an unmetaphysical age, it also supposes too great a distinction of quality between the empirical facts concerning the church and its significance in the purposes of God; a distinction of which, for example, a writing like the epistle to the Ephesians, which is undoubtedly idealistic about the church, shows little awareness. And not only too great a distinction, but a distinction of the wrong kind. Whatever the church's role truly is in mediating God to man, the mediation takes place only in the life which Christians in fact lead, in the words which at best stumble towards truth and the deeds which at best approximate to charity. It has no mode of action apart from those words and deeds. The distinction between the two levels which the Platonic-type theology deals in is best expressed not as two disparate truths about the church but as a truth about the church and a truth about God. In so far as he is to be known through the church, then that agency is, among other characteristics, both corrupt and fallible. To this we shall return.

The duality which these ways of thinking seek to face is present already in the church's earliest years. But nobody seems to have set himself to tackle it head on. In other words, it did not at this stage present itself as a problem demanding solution. The phenomenon could be observed and treated without its being regarded in that light. This does not mean that it was minimized. Rather, they looked at it in a perspective denied, in practice, to the great majority of their successors: that the end was near. This not only concentrates the mind wonderfully; it also shifts the proportions of things. At the coming end, the present disorders in Christian life will be speedily remedied. How it will be done is conceived of in a variety of ways – all of which amount to one thing: that God will join with himself the community of his chosen and perfected ones for eternal bliss. In the meantime, perhaps the mixed and ambiguous nature of the Christian community had better be tolerated (Matt. 13.30, 41), though extreme cases might be dealt with in a more drastic way (Matt. 18.17; I Cor. 5.5; Heb. 6.4ff.).

The believed imminence of the end gave the early church for a time a certain lightness of touch, a confidence, and a freedom from the need to dogmatize as it recognized the moral inadequacies of its members. Paul displays these qualities as he sees Christians simultaneously enjoying the most exalted status in the economy of God, and exhibiting imperfectly or even dismally its moral quality (Col. 3.1; Gal. 5.25; I Corinthians *passim*). Only the breathless nearness of the end can have made this inconsistency tolerable. God would soon deal with the untidiness of the present state of affairs.

In the first epistle of John, a further step has been taken. The distinction between the good and the bad in the church is now identified with the distinction between the orthodox and the heretical, and disagreement in doctrine has issued, for the first time in our knowledge, in actual schism (I John 2.19). In terms of the Johannine church, the schism represents a bifurcation on questions which the Fourth Gospel (taking it to be an earlier work) leaves unsettled; they had not then arisen with such rigour that decision was required. In the matter of eschatology, the gospel sees both a coming end (e.g. 6.39, 40, 44), and the fruits and values of the end as already present in Christ and his community (3.18f; 5.24). On the value of the created order, the gospel is both positive (1.1-3; 3.17) and negative (17.14, 16). With regard to the person of Christ, the gospel both sees him as real man (1.14), and presents him in general as a heavenly visitant in whom humanity is transcended. From the first epistle, it seems that on at least some of these issues, sharp division has now occurred. The 'heretics' do not believe that the Messiah was identical throughout with the human Jesus (4.2; 5.6); they believe that the fruits of the end have fully arrived, including sinlessness (1.7ff.). And while the 'orthodox' in fact share some of their convictions (e.g. on sin, 3.9, creating what appears to be inconsistency; and probably in taking a negative attitude to the created order, 2.15f.; 5.19), in other matters they have taken another option: the Messiah was fully human from start to finish, the end is near (2.18) and Christians, offspring of God though they are, still sin (5.16f.).

The bifurcation was forced, in so short a time, by the intellectual and religious pressures to which many Christian communities were subject as the first century gave place to the second

– broadly, the Gnostic movement. We observe it here in its opening stages, when the rival cases have still not reached full and clear formulation. The question is: what, ideally, ought to have happened? Is the balanced standpoint of the Fourth Gospel (as far as some of these issues are concerned) a 'perfect' presentation of the gospel such that it ought, if all had gone well, to have been preserved? Are we to criticize the first epistle for having, to a degree, upset the balance? But then is not our standard of judgment the fruit of our own theological preferences? We, perhaps, regard the gospel's sense of God's action as virtually completed, in Jesus (19.30) and his community, as preferable to the talk of an end still to come – which we may see as a piece of uncongenial Jewish mythology. Still, in the context of the Gnostic challenge, we may feel grateful that 'ordinary' Christianity, despite its (from our standpoint) rather crude way of expressing itself (for example in the matter of eschatology) stuck to its principles and refused to be drawn into the prevailing rejection of the material world, heady enjoyment of heaven-on-earth and dissolution of the uniqueness of Jesus into a welter of aeons. But when we enquire into our criteria for such a preference, it is difficult to be objective, for we stand too close to our own standards of truth and credibility.

Both in the earliest decades and in the succeeding period, witnessed to in the later New Testament writings, the church was an amalgam, even in the very heart of its faith, of local and transient circumstances and awareness of a commission entrusted to it. Though indeed the content of this commission can be stated in general terms (e.g. that Jesus, God's gift, in his life, death and resurrection is the key to new and authentic relationship with God), greater precision can only be gained by taking sides in disputed questions and choosing to emphasize one feature rather than another. The question quickly arises: if certain options are chosen, can the resulting faith be counted as authentically Christian, or has a perversion come into being, comparable to that brought about when Christians sin? In both cases, the image is blurred. The church no longer matches her claims to be the responsive instrument of God's purposes. Yet, in a changing world, adaptability is surely required of her: what are the criteria of legitimate adaptability?

Fundamentally, it is a matter of one's conviction about that changing world: whether it is essentially hostile, to be resisted by a faith which sets out to be immune and unchanging in the midst of it (apart from tactical moves); or essentially the object of God's loving and creative concern, so that the church must be constantly remoulded to fit into the pattern it provides. In other words, what is the true relationship between the gift of creation and the gift of the gospel? It is arguable that the remoulding always happens, in the long or the short run, whether the church is willing or not: so perhaps we ought to accept it in principle and begin our policy-making from that point.

Another New Testament example bears on the matter and raises the questions more acutely. The development of Pauline teaching and Pauline church life was in some respects comparable to that among Johannine Christians in the first century of the church's existence. The evidence lies on the one hand in Paul's genuine epistles and (for our present purpose) on the other hand in the Pastoral Epistles. To move from the one body of writings to the other is to go from an intense and positive awareness of a new and all-embracing gift of God in Christ which has revolutionized all life to a rather timid determination to preserve an orthodoxy whose terms are hardly stated, as if the fact of right belief were more important than the content. It is a move from a way of church life where there is intense awareness of the Spirit's gifts (e.g. I Cor. 12-14) to one where there is an anxious concern to establish proper organs of authority (I Tim. 3.1ff.; 4.12). It is a move from a world where moral behaviour flows straight from faith in Christ, as if under the pressure of that faith (Gal. 5.25), to one where rules and provisions must be laid out and where good conduct is almost an end in itself. Law (I Tim. 1.8) has reappeared as an unambiguous good and it is hard to avoid the sense that in many essential respects this Christianity is Judaism transposed into another key. Whatever the changes (for Jesus is certainly at the centre of the pattern of faith, e.g. I Tim. 2.5), the music often sounds much the same.

The mere description sounds like criticism. Yet to make it so is grossly unfair. For one has only to enter into the situation of the churches involved in the writing and receiving of the Pastoral Epistles to see how right and inevitable were the new concerns. In a church whose expectation of the end has not been fulfilled and which lacks central organization and direction, no wonder there is a determination to fix on criteria of orthodoxy and good government; no wonder there is a concern with the ordinary moral questions which arise in any human group. No wonder therefore that the distinctively Christian note is muted and that we are in the presence of an institution in many respects much like any other existing for comparable purposes. It is certainly, with necessary adjustments, recognizably the church we know. But what else could we expect?

In one sense we could expect nothing else. Yet we may still indicate a crucial point in the change which has occurred and draw conclusions. In theological discussion, we call it a change in the eschatological perspective. The Pauline epistles have a sense of God's work as already in train, indeed decisively inaugurated in Jesus. The new life of the Spirit, the essence of the longed-for resurrection, are available here and now. This awareness and the language which expressed it were the central piece of creative theology which distinguished the church from Judaism. By the time of the Pastoral Epistles it had to a large extent been lost; church life is now lived, faithfully and painstakingly, in expectation of the end which will, no doubt, come one day. The explanation for the change is quite simple: the earlier hope had been falsified in the simple and obvious sense.

Yet they were surely wrong to let this lead to a damping of ardour and a slackening of the sense of God's reality, so that questions of order and of moral regulation achieved a new and in a sense independent importance. From our standpoint, we may say that the essential theological point expressed in that primitive awareness of the end's imminence was a simple and intense conviction of God's gracious reality. That conviction was somehow overshadowed, it became less all-pervasive, less liberating, less the tune to which everything else must dance – and for no good theological reason: what good theological reason could there be? No doubt ardour cooled; the second generation had arrived. But there was no compelling reason for the change to express itself in a shift of emphasis and belief concerning the end, which was never the essential point. The essential point concerned the sense of the reality of God, but, alas, the two were hopelessly entangled together.

It may be that when that conviction truly informs Christian life and is the determinative substance of faith, then the outward shape of the church, even the statement of 'the faith' and even the moral behaviour of her members, are matters which in a sense can be trusted to take care of themselves. Or rather: if God be trusted in the world of his creating, then Christians are likely to err only interestingly and movingly (not, as generally, dully and flatly) in their witness to the gospel.

# 5

## *Good Liturgy or even Good Battlefield?*

Not surprisingly, controversy about the proposed new Holy Communion service* has centred on one clause: 'We offer this bread and this cup', said in the anamnesis section after the words of institution have been recited. This formula was accepted, no doubt with varying degrees of enthusiasm, by all except one of the members of the Liturgical Commission. But clearly the one dissident represents a substantial body of conservative Evangelical opinion which objects strongly to the words. This dissent is therefore significant and worth trying to meet in the cause of arriving at an agreed liturgy. It represents the first line of division which these words have caused. But it is not the only one. Objection also arises from people who are firmly Catholic in their general eucharistic theology but who find the formula an imperfect expression of it. This article sets out to elucidate and justify this point of view, lest it should be unthinkingly assumed that a Catholic doctrine of the eucharist is indissoluble from the words 'We offer this bread and this cup' or something very much like them. It would be a pity if their inclusion became a test and touchstone of Catholic orthodoxy in anybody's eyes.

The first issue is the broad one: is the action of the eucharist to be conceived as moving from God to man or from man to God? It is compatible with a manward view of the eucharist to see it as a spiritual feeding, a means of grace; but the Evangelical view which is chiefly propounded is more sophisticated and less satisfactory than this. It is to see the service as a recapitulation of the conversion experience. The worshipper reverently joins in a dramatic reliving of something which happened to him in the past and which was most clearly an act of God in his regard. Only when the act is complete (signified in the reception of the sac-

* The date was 1966 and the reference to the Second Series service as originally drafted.

rament) can he make the redeemed creature's offering and
response, in the shape of thanks and dedication to service. This
offering alone can rightly take place in the eucharist, as the 1662
rite suitably provides.

Evangelicals who see the eucharist thus no doubt find ample
opportunity to learn patience with those of us who cannot easily
share their picture! Not only does it seem strange that the particular action which is the eucharist should serve this kind of
dramatic purpose: were it not for the divine institution, one
would surely be tempted to say that other more suitable ways of
achieving this end are imaginable (e.g. the reading of the passion
story or the performing of a passion play). It is also hard to see
(once more, apart from its institution by Christ) how such a view
of the sacrament makes it *necessary* to salvation and to the Christian life or gives it a necessary place in the coherent scheme of
Christian theology.

But most of all: whereas the New Testament does give support
to a manward doctrine of the eucharist in the simple sense of a
feeding of man by God in the relationship already established by
God with him, it is hard to believe that the New Testament clearly
authenticates a doctrine which sees it as a recapitulation of the
experience of conversion: such a view would have to lean very
heavily indeed upon no more sure a support than one strand in
the meaning of the word *anamnesis*, together with one view of I
Cor. 11.26.

This is too narrow a way of basing eucharistic doctrine upon
the scriptures. That basis must be sought not in the first place in
eucharistic passages themselves but rather in a consideration of
the achieved work of Christ upon which the meaning of the
eucharist depends. Converted man shares in a corporate solidarity to which the New Testament writers witness in innum-
erable ways. Having by the divine initiative and gift alone
entered into the redeemed community, man has received a status
which is the given base for every subsequent Christian act. There
can be no question of needing to recapitulate this process as from
the position of one for whom it has not taken place. There is of
course a place in a Christian's prayers for the thankful remem-
brance of what God has done for us, but when we solemnly come
before God as in the eucharist we start from the firm reality of our
actual status. Every subsequent Christian act takes its place in
what is now the single responsive need and desire of the Christian soul: the offering of itself in thanksgiving and dedication for

service. Naturally, the eucharist *as a whole* shares that character. In other words, that which the Evangelical view sees as right and proper after the receiving of Communion is in fact the role of the whole Christian life, and therefore of course of the eucharist as a central act of that life. It is even *the* central act because its whole setting and symbolism are such as to typify the nature of Christian existence, with its several patterns of relationship (to God through Christ, to one's fellow-Christians in Christ) and with its essential qualities (because even its *mise en scène* expresses and evokes faith, hope and love).

It is important to begin by affirming that the setting of the whole Christian existence is 'in Christ' because it then follows easily that the purpose and direction of the eucharist will be identical with that of the whole Christian existence: that is, it will be ultimately Godward, because realization of union with God is the object of man's creation and redemption. This Godward look of man, the response of redeemed, converted man, can of course, like his whole existence, only be cast 'in Christ'. It is therefore done by no virtue of our own, but only through him. What Christ once did in the flesh provides the ever-existing basis for this acceptance of man into the divine relationship, in which Christ is eternally the self-giving one, as he was once at the flesh-level on Calvary.

So it is a question of Christ offering himself to the Father (what else can we say to express the nature of the perfect love which constitutes the divine life?) and us by sheer grace participating in that offering – in life as a whole, and so *ipso facto*, and for the very purpose of saying it, doing it, sacramentally, in the eucharist.

Even that simple manward view which sees the eucharist as a simple feeding of the Christian cannot be left there. For what is the purpose of this feeding but our union with God, the fulfilment of the end of our creation?

It is clear that the bare Godward/manward distinction is crude and inadequate when applied to eucharistic doctrine. Of course the whole initiative is God's: but man responds – yet only in and through Christ; and man's goal is God.

It is a doctrinal approach of this kind which causes dissatisfaction with 'We offer this bread and this cup'. Simply, it does not truthfully say in plain English what is taking place. We do not, strictly, offer to God bread and cup, for what could God want with these or any other gifts of ours? ('Nothing in my hand I bring, simply to thy cross I cling': here we join hands with the

Evangelical.) Admittedly, the words are a kind of shorthand: a liturgy is not and cannot be expected to be a watertight doctrinal treatise. But then surely we can find a better shorthand than this, one that more immediately conveys its proper sense. For *we* do not offer in our own right: *Christ* offers – in one way, once for all on Calvary, in another, different but consistent way, eternally. Nor do we offer *bread and wine*: Christ offers *himself*. And we do not offer Christ (for whom 'bread and cup' stand): again, Christ offers himself – and we by grace through faith participate. The whole act of giving thanks over and receiving bread and wine is the means whereby this is 'earthed' – brought into history and human life: it is the whole act, its total setting and symbolism, which does this, not any single part of it.

The section of the eucharistic prayer in its traditional form (and in the revised service) which most adequately expresses this, giving a skeleton-like résumé of the whole doctrinal pattern, is the doxology, which is no mere formula to give a sonorous lead into the Amen, but the key expression of what is being done, so that the people of God can fittingly give their assent. The action of the eucharist, like all Christian life, is directed to the Father, through Christ, in the Spirit-led life of the church.

The arguments in favour of 'We offer this bread and this cup' seem to many Catholic-minded Anglicans to be formidable. There is no doubt that the universal tradition of the ancient liturgies is in favour of it (or some equivalent), and well-loved hymns embody it. Liturgists with one voice (so it appears) support it. They can be accused of patristic fundamentalism. They can reply that what they are urging is the universal tradition from the earliest period in which any tradition at all becomes visible and that a witness of such strength should not lightly be disregarded. The evidence from early and continuous tradition – and also from numerous modern revisions, some of them in firmly Protestant quarters, so that the English Evangelical protest seems oddly parochial – is firmly on their side.

It can also be held that the tradition of 'offering-language' derives from scripture – though by canons of biblical interpretation no longer readily acceptable to any of the parties in the present discussions. Much of it comes from what seemed in the first centuries a natural typology and fulfilment of prophecy: the old covenant had its sacrifices, and so did the new, as foretold in Mal. 1.11, a verse which was so marvellously fulfilled in the world-wide celebration of the eucharist. If we now find some

difficulty in yielding support to this way of using the Old Testament as a foreshadowing of the fuller revelation, some doubt is
cast on the authority of formulae which began their Christian
career on the basis of it – in particular, 'We offer this bread and
this cup'. It is a typology whose elements have not passed fully
through the single prism of Christ's person.

We have been appealing against the letter of tradition to what is
in effect that third strand in Christian authority – the reasonable
and credible demands of a consistent doctrine. We have also
appealed to scripture, and we have hoped to imply that this
doctrine springs from and is demanded by the full scriptural
teaching which is relevant to the question. This teaching is not so
narrow as the consideration of the passages which directly concern the eucharist or the Last Supper, but it stretches out into
more fundamental matters, as indeed does the very language of
those passages themselves (e.g. terms like 'covenant', 'my body',
etc.). The doctrine of the eucharist is a dependent doctrine and
cannot be approached as if it ought to stand on its own feet. It
rests upon doctrine concerning christology, the work of Christ,
the church, the nature of the Christian life, and baptism perhaps
most pertinently in the context of our present disputings. It is no
wonder that treatment merely of eucharistic texts in scripture is
liable to be both insufficient and even harmful.

Of course, a liturgy need not set out to provide a full and
precise statement of the doctrine held by those who form and use
it, but it should do the best it can, especially to provide a shorthand which evokes the best possible images and refrains from
misleading pointers. 'We offer this bread and this cup' seems not
to satisfy these requirements. A new liturgy does not only owe a
debt to the Christian past (and liturgies have not, historically,
ever been particularly reliable guards against their own mis-
interpretation!). It also owes a debt to the present – to Christian
doctrine at its widest, as the Spirit teaches us. And a debt to the
present also in the sense that no Christian statement in our day,
whether doctrinal or even liturgical, however much it belongs to
the intimate life of the Christian community, can or ought to
avoid wholly the character of apologetic. It must be as directly
intelligible as possible to men who do not think even about
Christian things in a ghetto of theological ideas and full of respect
for Christian antiquity. To-day's tools make it right and proper to
improve upon antiquity where we can.

Finally, it is important when it is a question of disagreement between various groups in the church, that the disputes should be fixed at the right points. 'We offer this bread and this cup' so much fails to express accurately Catholic eucharistic doctrine that while it can be expected that Catholics will bear with it and even like it, from long familiarity (while mentally interpreting it, we hope in a fully satisfactory sense), it cannot reasonably be expected that others, for whom it has no such associations and for whom its plain meaning is, not unreasonably, repugnant should accept it. If we disagree, let us disagree on theology and on points of substance. The better placed the disagreement, the stronger the chance of ultimate harmony or at least of willing sympathy.

# 6

## *Sacrifice and the Eucharist*[1]

The aim of this essay is to clarify a cloudy area in the landscape of Christian theology; then to see whether the name by which it has traditionally been known, eucharistic sacrifice, remains a candidate for survival. We begin by examining the substructure of the problem: what makes talk of sacrifice in relation to the eucharist so laden with difficulty? This leads to the question: what was there in Jewish sacrificial institutions that brought this language into play in relation to Christ and his acts? The third and longest section of the essay is devoted to an attempt to disentangle the great number of conceptual threads in the use of sacrificial language in eucharistic theology in the course of the church's history. Finally, we face the question: what needs to be said? Does the language of sacrifice aid the saying of it?

### 1. *The Substructure*

Most obviously, difficulty arises because the image of sacrifice is no longer current coin. The institution belongs, as far as Christian use is concerned, to ancient Israel, and parallels in currently flourishing religions have only a rather remote anthropological interest for Christians living in the West and indeed in many other parts of the world.

But while this difficulty reduces the vividness of the language, it is partly curable by instruction. More serious is the fact that as we survey the history of Christian doctrine we find that there is no one, clearly identifiable entity which we can label 'the doctrine of eucharistic sacrifice'. As we shall see, the term has covered a wide variety of ideas, many of them having hardly any relation to each other and operating along quite distinct logical lines. So we have to ask: what precisely is being discussed when this terminology is used?

It is common in discussion of this, as of other theological topics,

for hidden Platonist assumptions to cause much needless confusion, and the fact that a particular phrase has had a number of
different senses sometimes merely intensifies the tenacity with
which these assumptions are held. The supposed objective existence of something called 'the eucharistic sacrifice' easily diverts
attention from haziness about the meaning. Statements such as 'I
understand *the* eucharistic sacrifice thus and thus' or 'I see *it* so
and so' conceal the fact that the term is being stretched to cover a
wide range of concepts, and that distinctions are crying out to be
made.

This diversity of sense is of course a feature, to one degree or
another, of the history of every Christian doctrine. There are, for
instance, many christologies, many doctrines of the atonement.
But in the case of eucharistic sacrifice, it is accentuated by uncertainty as to what precisely is at stake. We may draw a contrast.
Thus, in the case of christology, it is clear that whatever formulation is adopted, it is an attempt to give an account of the
belief that in the person of Jesus there is a special or unique
meeting of divine and human. In the case of the atonement, there
is always an attempt to show how Christ's work may be understood as restoring alienated man to relationship with God. That is
what christology and atonement doctrine are about. In the case of
eucharistic sacrifice, there is no comparably specific task. It is
simply that Christians have traditionally used the language of
sacrifice in relation to the eucharist, though their intention in
doing so has been to give expression to a wide range of quite
distinct ideas concerning the sacrament.

We shall see that the ideas which enter into the discussion of
this doctrine include some that are not strictly theological at all,
and some that depend upon the wording of a particular biblical or
liturgical text, written usually with other purposes in mind. It is
not hard to see why eucharistic doctrine has displayed this lux-
uriant quality to a far greater degree than, for example, christology or atonement doctrine. It has had to make its way through
the conceptually loose growth of liturgical and devotional formulae as well as the more tightly controlled paths marked out by
councils and theologians. In sum, 'eucharistic sacrifice' has
covered a multifarious variety of ideas which have in common
little more than (*a*) some element of Godward movement of
thought or aspiration, and (*b*) a link with some aspect of the
eucharist. A number of them have had little to do with what we
shall refer to as the central eucharistic 'area', that is the features,

grounded in the Last Supper, which distinguish the eucharist from other rites and acts. Nevertheless, it is not right to suppose that the idea of sacrifice has been imposed upon the eucharist: rather, it has been drawn out of it – in a variety of ways, some more appropriate than others.

## 2. *The Background*

The language of sacrifice came into Christian vocabulary from the already diversified practice of Judaism. There, sacrificial rites ranged from the peace offerings (in which the animal was partly burned on the altar as 'food offered by fire for a pleasing odour' and partly consumed by the people, in a fellowship meal between God and his people) to sin offerings and burnt offerings (in which there was no meal, and the rite signified total consecration to God, or, in the case of the former, brought release from sin). Passover, which lay more immediately in the background of Christ's death and so of the Last Supper, though not itself a rite belonging to any of these categories, combined a number of their themes. The eating of this meal in Jewish households was the expression *par excellence* of the harmonious communion between Israel and God. It expressed the proper and total allegiance of the people to God their redeemer; and it saw this as grounded in this historic act of deliverance from Egypt.

It was not long before the first Christians, experiencing reconciliation to God as a result of Christ's life, death and resurrection, began to interpret their experience in the language closest to hand, that of sacrifice. The underlying logic was simple: reconciliation had taken place, sacrifices reconcile, so Christ's work, the occasion and basis of the reconciliation, must be interpreted sacrificially. There was less agreement about the precise application of this range of imagery. The New Testament writers show three chief patterns. Attention naturally focused on Christ's death (for sacrificial victims die), and it was easy to see it as the once for ever effective sin-offering (e.g. Rom. 3.24f.). If, as in the Epistle to the Hebrews, the ritual of the Day of Atonement was chosen as the model, then Christ's sacrifice was seen as consummated at his entry into heaven, by analogy with the high priest entering the holy of holies in the temple. In the gospels (e.g. in the symbolism of the Fourth Gospel and perhaps in Mark 10.45), Jesus' death was not surprisingly seen in the light of the Passover rite, for it occurred at the time of the feast: it effected perfectly and universally what that rite signified for Israel – a profound deliverance from all bondage, to be completed in the messianic kingdom. But whatever the pattern, it comes to this: that God was seen to have acted in Christ in a manner most satisfactorily expounded in sacrificial terms, and this act had met and made realizable the desire of alienated man for fellowship with his Creator.

It was the most natural thing in the world that the liturgical act, whereby Christ's death is recalled and made once more vivid to his people, and whereby eternal fellowship with God is anticipated, should also attract to itself sacrificial language and imagery. What is perhaps surprising is the tortuous and complex way in which this has often been done. This will be apparent, as we go on to examine the story of the church's use of the idea of sacrifice in connection with the eucharist.

## 3. *The Story*

What now follows is not primarily intended to be a chronological summary of the history of ideas in relation to eucharistic sacrifice, but rather a survey of the different patterns of thought which have arisen in this area. For the sake of clarity, we shall occasionally sharpen distinctions a little unfairly. The chief aim is to provide analysis. The result will be threefold. First, to rule some of the ideas out of strictly doctrinal discussion altogether – they belong in the less rigorous sphere of aids to devotion. Whether they are misleading or helpful is a question to be judged by other criteria, those proper to that sphere. Second, to show some as so wedded to outdated or barren conceptual and symbolic patterns as to be more than ready for relegation to the museum for religious period-pieces. Third, to make clearer the terms on which discussion can now usefully be conducted.

The following list of twelve distinguishable strands is unlikely to be exhaustive. But it may be long enough both for the reader's patience and to demonstrate the main point of this essay.

1. *First signs.* The root of the matter is in Mal. 1.11, a text which speedily commended itself to Christian expositors who saw the fulfilment of the Old Testament in the deeds of Christ and the preaching of the church. It does not appear in any of the New Testament books, but was certainly in use before the last of them was written. The verse is: 'From the rising of the sun to its setting my name is great among the nations, and in every place incense is

offered to my name, and a pure offering; for my name is great among the nations, says the Lord of hosts.'

It makes its first appearance in the *Didache of the Twelve Apostles* (ch.14), where the stress is on the need for a *pure* sacrifice and the quotation backs an exhortation not to take part in the eucharist until personal differences have been settled. Moral purity is a prerequisite for worship. There is no stress whatsoever on the term 'sacrifice' itself, and the context is not theological but hortatory. This writer's typical way of describing the eucharist is as the breaking of bread and the giving of thanks (cf. also *Did.* 9). Nevertheless, the text – and the word 'sacrifice' – had gained a foothold in Christian speech about the eucharist.

In other writers, the text comes into prominence for three other reasons. In the first place, it was part of a set of Old Testament passages with liturgical connections, which were seen as foretelling in various ways the contrast between the purely Jewish old Israel, with its inadequate worship, and the new universal church. The use of Isa. 56.7 (cf. also Jer. 7.11) in Mark 11.17 is perhaps the first instance of this: 'My house shall be called a house of prayer for all the nations.' The vein came to be richly worked, for example, in the second century, in Justin's *Dialogue with Trypho* (41,117), where, in addition to use of the Malachi text, it is explored in relation to circumcision and the sabbath. In the second place, the text enables a writer like Justin to underline the providential universality of the church. The fact that it was possible to point to a contrast, between Israel's sacrifice confined to Jerusalem and the church's which was found 'in every place', enabled Justin to bypass a fact inconvenient for apologetic – that Jews as well as Christians were to be found throughout the cities of the Roman world (cf. also Irenaeus, *Against Heresies* IV.17.5).

In the third place, the theme of sacrifice forms one element in a typological scheme which speedily emerged in the thought-patterns of the early church. By this, the people of the new covenant are seen to possess a set of 'equipment' parallel at each point to that possessed by the people of the old. In this case, it is as if it was said: 'they had their sacrifices, we have ours, for sacrifice is part of the providentially ordered scheme'. This line of thought is first worked out at the end of the first century in the *First Epistle of Clement* (40.4), which also includes the similar parallel between the priesthood of Israel and the officers of the church: 'The High Priest has his own proper services assigned to him. . . . In the same way, my brothers, when we offer our own

Eucharist to God, each one of us should keep to his own degree.'
A century later, Irenaeus repeats the argument: 'There were
oblations there [among the Jews], and there are oblations here
[among the Christians]' (IV.18.2). It is evident that it is the presence of sacrifices in the religious institutions of Israel which
impels the application of this language to the most closely comparable element among the institutions of the church, to wit, the
eucharist, rather than anything demanded by the nature of the
eucharist itself. The argument began with the old rather than the
new, and the old called the tune.

The most interesting feature of the early uses of this text is that
from the point of view of doctrinal thinking and the emergence of
a concept of eucharistic sacrifice, every one of these aspects is
quite incidental. Of all the elements in Mal. 1.11, the idea of
sacrifice in itself was the least explored of all, in the period when it
was so prominently employed. It may not be going too far to say
that in many cases, the term 'sacrifice' carries little or nothing of
its technical sense. It signifies hardly more than *Gottesdienst*,
*l'office*, *religious service* do with us, that is, it is the quite general
term for an act of religious worship and does not indicate any
particular way of looking at the eucharist.

2. *Offering gifts.* From early times, the element of sacrifice in
the eucharist has been seen in terms of 'offering the gifts'. It
seems to have arisen as part of the typological pattern which we
referred to above (p. 69). Its first appearance was in *I Clement* 44.4,
where, quite casually it seems, the essential office of the bishop is
described in these terms: 'For we shall be guilty of no slight sin if
we eject from the episcopate men who have offered the gifts
blamelessly and holily.' Once more then the language of sacrifice
is a subsidiary feature. It was nourished by the appeal to other
Old Testament texts besides Mal. 1.11, in particular Deut. 16.16.
This appears, for example, in Irenaeus (*Against Heresies* IV.18.1):
'We are bound, therefore, to offer to God the firstfruits of his
creation, as Moses also says, "Thou shalt not appear in the
presence of the Lord thy God empty-handed"; so that man,
being accounted as grateful, by those things in which he has
shown his gratitude, may receive that honour which flows from
him.' (Cf. also Justin's seeing of the Jewish offering of fine flour
by those purified from leprosy as a foreshadowing of the
eucharistic bread, *Dialogue with Trypho* 41.)

Without this typological frame of mind, it is hard to see how the
idea would have come into the eucharist 'area', with which it is

not at all integrally connected. At no point does it link conceptually with the eucharist's central concern, that is, with the Lord's death and resurrection and his people's status in relation to him. The typological mentality created a feeling of deep inner appropriateness, linking old offering with new, which pushed its way to the surface in reflection upon the eucharist, as upon other matters. The rite was, after all, one might say, the most likely candidate within Christian practice for such treatment in relation to this theme. But it is so unspecifically eucharistic that it could equally appropriately be attached to quite other Christian devotions, e.g. harvest festivals or gift days. Moreover, the insistent objection presents itself, that God has no need of our gifts and that the underlying conception is, from the point of view of Christian belief about God, crude and mistaken. Nevertheless, once this idea had found an entry into Christian thought on the eucharist, it was hard to dislodge, and has had enthusiastic revivals in recent years.

3. *Firstfruits of creation.* This is a special form of the idea which we have just examined and suffers from the same defects. But it brings its own special associations. The bread and wine are presented to God as the first instalments of a creation, which one day will be wholly rejuvenated. Irenaeus expresses it thus (IV.18.4): 'For it behoves us to make an oblation to God, and in all things to be found grateful to God our Maker, in a pure mind, and in faith without hypocrisy, in well-grounded hope, and in fervent love, offering the firstfruits of his own created things.' He goes on to attack those who see the created order as having issued from 'apostasy, ignorance and passion', in these words: 'How can they be consistent with themselves, when they say that the bread over which thanks have been given is the body of their Lord, and the cup his blood, if they do not call him the Son of the creator of the world, that is, his Word, through whom the wood fructifies, and the fountains gush forth, and the earth gives "first the blade, then the ear, then the full corn in the ear".'

Obviously this idea is full of rich devotional content. But it is only marginally linked with the meaning of the eucharist and has no clear connection with the idea of sacrifice in relation to the eucharistic 'area', as we defined it on p. 67.

4. *The offering of Christ's body and blood.* A successor to and crucial variant of the idea of *offering gifts* arises when, in Cyprian, the notion of offering is weaned from its predominantly typological context and attached more closely to other – and more central

– aspects of eucharistic belief, in particular the presence in the sacrament of Christ's body and blood. The fusion results, as it were haphazardly, in the following concept: that of offering to God as our gifts the body and blood of Christ.[2]

From the point of view of the logic of doctrine, this is the key moment in the development of the idea of eucharistic sacrifice. Ideas about Godward offering, making use, as we have seen, of a variety of sacrificial notions, mostly drawn from the Old Testament, but all of them peripheral to the content and meaning of the eucharist, now win a place in the centre of the picture, through the association of sacrificial language with 'body and blood' language. The latter had so far had a separate history and had always belonged to the very heart of the eucharistic 'area'.

Yet surely this marriage was a mistake. The life and death of Jesus are past events. Jesus offered himself on the cross. Present Christian life is 'in Christ', and is offered to God only by its relation to Christ's *self*-offering. It could never do justice to those facts and ideas to describe any Christian act as *our* offering of Christ's body and blood to the Father. It presented the relationship of Christ and Christian as too external and inevitably threatened to treat the 'body and blood' as objects that can be handled. Moreover, it failed to do full justice to the eucharist as the expression of an already existing relationship of the believers with God through Christ. It is all the more tragic, then, that all subsequent development was to be within the context of this fusion and to be bedevilled by it. However widely thought about eucharistic sacrifice was to range, it always stayed within the terms which it laid down – whether by way of working out its implications in the light of some new doctrinal emphasis or intellectual setting, or by way of reaction against it.

5. *Propitiation and satisfaction.* Under the former heading (i.e., the working out of the implications of the idea of *offering Christ's body and blood*) we may place the most important new emphasis of the succeeding period. It is the effect upon eucharistic belief of that stringent sense of God's justice and its requirements which is associated particularly with the name of Anselm (though it goes back much earlier, even perhaps to Cyprian, the lawyer turned bishop), and which is best seen as one element in a general concern in the medieval period with the establishing and defining of legal rights and obligations. Once the whole question of Christ's redemptive work was set in the context of a God whose inflexible justice was an overriding characteristic, the sacrifice of

the eucharist was bound to take on a new aspect and to raise new questions. Fresh elements in the ample stock (from both scripture and the Christian tradition) of sacrificial terminology pressed to the forefront of men's minds.

In particular, there was the question of the relationship between the past, all-sufficing act of satisfaction for sin made on the cross and the repeated act of the eucharist. The two acts clearly bore so many of the same characteristics, and demanded to be spoken of in closely similar terms. Above all, both alike were rich in sacrificial associations. How, then, was the relationship to be defined? Could the first avail for man by means of the second? In the search for definition, various possibilities were exploited. The three leading ones may be expressed in the form of propositions: (i) 'The daily sacrifice is a *memorial* of the *Passion*' (Paschasius Radbertus, ninth century); (ii) 'Christ is daily immolated *mystically*' (ibid.); (iii) The eucharist is an *unbloody* sacrifice. The italicized words show the points at which the statement is most vulnerable or ambiguous, as if it were attempting at the same time to say and refrain from saying, working towards identity but not quite affirming it. In each case, the concern is to establish both the connection and the distinction between the cross and the eucharist, the one 'sacrifice' and the other. In the light of later controversy (from the fifteenth century onwards), the first way of expressing this (in terms of *memorial*) looks a good deal weaker than the other two; but it is not clear that when they were first formulated it was seen as essentially different from them.

All these expressions bear chiefly on the *kind* of sacrifice that the eucharist was thought to be. There was also the question of how the sacrifice was to be seen to work. How did the past act affect present life, and how did the eucharist operate to that end? There were two chief lines of approach. The first and older was in terms of *propitiation*. Taken from Jewish precedents, it was applied (or taken to have been applied) to the death of Jesus in the teaching of St Paul and St John (Rom. 3.25 and I John 2.2). It had been applied to the eucharist from the time of Cyril of Jerusalem in the fourth century. In the context of the medieval assumptions, questions and demands, this was the most appropriate category available within the traditional theological vocabulary of sacrifice.

But more immediate to men's minds, and more powerful psychologically, was the category of satisfaction, with its roots in the assumptions of society, in particular those of feudalism. Men were deeply conscious that in coming before the all-holy, perfectly just God, payment must be made of all outstanding dues. Man could not come to God without the required payment for his sins – or a commutation of it. Just as knight-service could be commuted into a money payment, so the sacrifice of Christ could be commuted into the offering of the eucharist elements.

In a variant of the same idea, the sacrifice could be offered with a view to achieving certain objects; for the forgiveness of sins, or for the obtaining of specified benefits. As the history of the Roman canon shows, this approach indeed antedated both the atonement theory of Anselm which gave it the most comprehensive formal backing and the social system whose demands made it so fitting.[3] By this time, the eucharist had long been regarded by many as an *effective* sacrifice, with purchasing power for the needs of both the living and the dead. Once more, this was a feature in eucharistic thinking that was peripheral to the rite's distinctive and central significance, for intercession, thanksgiving and penitence can be expressed quite apart from the eucharist. But that act was felt to be the occasion when the worshipper could with most confidence bring his petitions, for it was his closest approach to the heart of the majesty of God. Christ, who had made the perfect sacrifice, would plead its merits, as the worshipper's friendly advocate at the heavenly court.

6. *The sacrifice of Jesus: human and once for all*. The Reformers, and indeed to some degree their predecessors, reacted strongly against many of these concepts and against the whole ethos of theology to which they belonged. There was, of course, a reaffirmation of scriptural ideas. But behind that, their approach may be described as fundamentally humanistic. This was true in two senses. First, it was literary before it was conceptual: there was an attempt to let the texts, chiefly scriptural but also patristic, give their plain meaning. Second, it was concerned with Christ the man or – more formally – Christ's humanity. Thus, for example, Erasmus' teaching on the eucharist focuses chiefly on the believer's assimilation into mind and heart of the inspiring personal example of Jesus. Though the leading Reformers used more conceptual categories, they were nevertheless deeply influenced by this tendency. Hence their concern (so literalistic, as it often seems to us) with the present location of Christ's human (though glorified) body, and their difficulty in seeing that the central eucharistic language involved a multiplicity of senses, each shad-

ing into another. Hence, too, their stress on spiritual (which we might almost translate 'imaginative' – their tendency moves theology somewhat in the direction of poetry) communion with Christ in the receiving of the sacrament. And hence the viewing of the eucharist as a kind of passion play which revitalizes saving faith in the believer by making possible the devout recalling of Christ's death. In this last line of thought, common in Lutheran piety, we find once more something which is peripheral to the eucharist in itself: if this is what it signifies, then a sermon or a dramatic production will serve as well. The eucharist becomes an enacted preaching of the word. If not dispensable in practice (for the Lord instituted it), it is hard to see it as essential in theory.

But alongside these developments, the Reformers also worked within the terms of the existing scholastic ideas. The question of the relationship between the sacrifice of Calvary and that of the altar remained a live one. Only now, because of the more vivid sense of scripture and of Christ's human life and death, awareness of the uniqueness and all-sufficiency of the cross was so dominant that the eucharist had to be denied its sacrificial character (in the traditional senses) altogether. In the light of the new sensitivity, traditional formulations bristled with difficulties. Two of the three propositions which we listed under 5 (p. 73) – 'Christ is daily immolated mystically' and 'the eucharist is an unbloody sacrifice' – now seemed to fail to make the distinction between cross and eucharist anything like sharp enough. *Memorial*, however, remained acceptable, and was the term which most clearly linked old teaching and new. To see the eucharist as a memorial of Calvary made no inroads upon either the pastness or the uniqueness of Christ's sacrificial death. Still, there were changes, even in this area. Whereas formerly the eucharist had been 'the memorial sacrifice', now it became 'the memorial of the sacrifice'. At the verbal level, much came to turn on the delicate oscillation (first found as long ago as Tertullian) between *representation* and *re-presentation*. We may note, for example, Ridley's admission in 1555 that the eucharist 'is offered after a certain manner, and in a mystery, and as a representation of that bloody sacrifice; and he doth not lie, who saith Christ to be so offered'. To say that was to go as far as possible to meet traditionally-minded opponents (when one was on trial for one's life).

Because the whole way of conceiving the leading theological categories had become more realistic and humanistic, certain old ways of thinking were now quite excluded. Thus, for Calvin, to speak of an unbloody sacrifice was nonsense: the very notion of sacrifice involved death and blood-shedding. 'Sacrifice' meant something quite definite and vivid, so the traditional phrase was a contradiction in terms. Similarly, because Christ's glorified body is in heaven, here below all we can possibly do concerning his death is to commemorate it – and that is a very luminous and strong thing to do. Not surprisingly, Calvin can say that the (old) mass positively erases 'the true and unique death of Christ' and (here is the point) 'drives it from the memory of man'. Memory is the faculty relevant to the matter, and we remember by giving sole attention to the factual death of Calvary that happened once, long ago (*Institutes* IV.18.5). Other Reformers, like Zwingli, write in similar vein.

7. *The sacrifice of praise*. Not that the Reformers eliminated all use of sacrificial language. Quite the contrary, some old phrases now received a new lease of life. Far from trying to dam up all talk of sacrifice in relation to the eucharist, they preferred to divert it into satisfactory channels. Apart from the emphasis on the eucharist as the memorial of Christ's unique sacrifice (thus making the eucharist itself firmly a non-sacrifice), the term occurs in three other shapes. First, the sacrifice of praise and thanksgiving.

This phrase had a venerable history, notably in the canon of the Roman mass; but now it was used for a purpose to which it was admirably suited, the decontamination of the sacrificial idea. For its effect was to place the eucharist firmly on a level with all other Christian acts of prayer and worship. This purpose was quite deliberate. Thus, Bucer wrote in 1545 that when the Fathers called the eucharist 'the offering of Christ' they meant the offering of prayer and praise, and that these sacrifices 'ought to be found in all holy assemblies, even though the holy supper be not celebrated in them'. The same line is followed by the English Reformers, like Cranmer and Ridley.[4] This phraseology was intended to restore to the idea of sacrifice its proper place in relation to Christian worship. But inevitably, because of the polemical context, it could hardly appear other than negative in its bearing on eucharistic doctrine. While it at least witnessed to the 'offering', Godward character of all Christian worship, including the eucharist, it failed to give any satisfactory account of the eucharist's specific place within it.

8. *The sacrifice of selves*. The Reformers also applied sacrificial language to the worshippers' offering of themselves to God. This was a more positive doctrine, for it was specifically connected

with the eucharist's distinctive and central features. But it is important to note what it affirmed and what it rejected. There was no question of the believers' offering themselves to God in the perfect offering of Christ, made present (however that might be seen) in the eucharist. Rather, by receiving the sacrament, the believers enacted the memorial of the sacrifice of Calvary, and in the strength of that outward sign were then (and then only) able to offer themselves to God for his service. It is essentially a post-communion offering (see the first post-communion prayer in the Book of Common Prayer of 1552 and 1662). The sacrifice is the communicant's devout response to the gift bestowed upon him in the sacrament. It does not consist of the sacramental elements themselves and is not connected with the consecration of the elements.

Behind this idea lies the Protestant sense of the centrality of faith in the all-sufficiency of Christ's sacrifice, a faith renewed by the experience of the rehearsal of Christ's passion in the eucharist. Faith renewed leads directly to the renewal of self-offering.

Though its context is certainly eucharistic, it must be said that this theme, like that of the offering of praise, is not worked closely into a coherent pattern of specifically eucharistic doctrine. Self-offering is what is primarily in view; the eucharist is simply one among a number of contexts in which it may be expressed and reaffirmed.

9. *The sacrifice of alms*. In replacing old ideas of eucharistic sacrifice, the Reformers discerned not only a sacrifice of praise and a sacrifice of selves, but also a sacrifice of gifts in the shape of the alms of the people. Conceptually, this raises nothing fresh: it is simply 2 above (p. 70) put into a new context.

What is more interesting about the Reformers' formulations on this subject is the way in which broadly Platonist assumptions still governed the matter. It was taken for granted that there was such a thing as 'sacrifice in the eucharist', only Catholic theologians discerned it mistakenly. The task of theology was to formulate it correctly, and the procedure, in effect, was to discover, if possible on ancient precedent, features of the true (i.e. Reformed) eucharistic theology to which sacrificial language could suitably be applied.

This same mode of thought has also been apparent at the merely verbal level, particularly in high Anglican teaching. Sometimes it seems that writers have been as it were bemused by the word 'sacrifice' itself, and have felt impelled to draw into a single pattern of thought every approved use of the word in eucharistic contexts, whether from early Christian writers, or from liturgies of past or present. The result has tended to be statements which, however stimulating they may be devotionally, defy attempts to reduce them to logical coherence.[5]

10. *The sacrifice of the church*. The Reformation insistence upon the offering of 'ourselves, our souls and bodies' has a more Catholic counterpart in the idea of the offering of the church. Both Roman Catholic and Anglican theologians (notably R. I. Wilberforce) have contributed to its elaboration.

Whatever the resemblances, the conceptual setting is quite different from the comparable Protestant doctrine. It stems from the Pauline and Johannine teaching about life 'in Christ', and found typical formulation in relation to the eucharist in St Augustine's words: 'Since the Church is his body, she learns through him to offer herself' (*De Civitate Dei* X.20). It revived when there was a slackening (chiefly in this century) of a strict application to the eucharist of the categories of propitiation and satisfaction. Characteristically, it is expressed in terms of the body offering itself in the eucharist, in Christ the head, to the Father. In effect, it is an application to the eucharist context of the ecclesiology of the Epistle to the Ephesians. This pattern has the merit of binding the idea of sacrifice in the eucharist to more fundamental doctrine, neglect of which is only too apparent in so many of the other patterns. It sets the eucharist, seen as a firmly Godward act, firmly in the setting of christology and ecclesiology. Its weakness is a too rigid dependence upon the particular image of the body of Christ.[6]

11. *The heavenly altar*. Seventeenth-century Anglicanism was also responsible for bringing another ancient idea into new prominence: that of the heavenly altar at which Christ's once-for-all sacrifice is eternally pleaded, while, in dependent parallelism, the church militant offers its eucharistic worship at the earthly altar (as once, provincial ceremonies mirrored those of the imperial court in Rome). This affords a pictorial framework within which a number of the other concepts may be seen; it does not conflict with other ideas but combines with them relatively easily. This of course is also the root of its weakness. Its ineradicably pictorial and analogical character makes it hard to fit into a more abstract conceptual pattern, if coherence is to be maintained.

The roots of it are so distinguished and comprehensive that it was bound to become prominent. They range from the Epistle to the Hebrews, through patristic texts and the Roman canon to the Protestant emphasis on the all-sufficiency of Calvary. It was a satisfying doctrine for those (like the seventeenth-century high Anglicans) who wished to give more positive content to the traditional, above all patristic, sacrificial teaching in relation to the eucharist, while, at least to their own satisfaction, not abandoning their Protestant heritage. Protestantism itself has remained unconvinced by a model which seems to threaten the uniqueness of Calvary.

12. *Liturgy as the biography of Christ.* Among all the ways in which the eucharist has been thought of in sacrificial terms, this is both eccentric and conceptually independent of all the rest. It is the notion of the form of the liturgy itself as a retracing of the steps of the life, death and resurrection of Christ. Used mainly as a devotional aid, it naturally depends wholly on what are from this point of view the accidents of liturgical development. Thus, the pattern works when the *Gloria in Excelsis* is at the beginning of the Mass, to represent the nativity, but not when it comes at the end. According to this view, the canon contains, after the recital of the story of the Supper, the offering of the sacrifice – the rehearsal of Calvary. This scheme serves to accentuate the realism of a quasi-identification of Calvary and eucharist, to which other patterns also lead. So it gained a certain amount of rather dubious support.

## 4. *Sacrifice and the Eucharist*

What conclusions emerge from this disentangling of threads? The analysis is in some ways discouraging. The first entry of the term 'sacrifice' into discussions of the eucharist was, from the point of view of its central meaning, tangential. Its use in the course of Christian history has often been peripheral or positively mistaken. Peripheral in the sense that it has brought out features of the eucharist that belong to the conceptually less strict sphere of piety or are anyhow incidental to the rite's main significance. Mistaken in the sense that some of the most common lines of thought on the subject fail to do justice to the christology, soteriology and ecclesiology upon which surely sound eucharistic doctrine ought to rest.

But there is another side to the matter. The very fact that sacrificial language has been so persistent in thought about the eucharist, the very fact that it has taken so many different and often original turns indicates that, however tortuous or muddled the thought has often been, 'sacrifice' is a useful and perhaps indispensable concept in this connection. There are grounds for declining to be wholly discouraged from its use. Chiefly, 'sacrifice' has one property which other images lack and which needs to be included in any account of the believer's relationship with God: totality of self-offering. It is true that the term is no longer current coin. It is also true that some uses of it have neglected this very feature which is its strength (e.g. the idea of the eucharist as a sacrifice of praise and thanksgiving). Nevertheless, this remains its most useful feature, for how else can man come before God except in the attitude of sacrifice and with the intention to offer all? The question is, how ought this to be articulated in relation to the eucharist? How may the image be suitably exploited? And how can it be brought into relation to Christ's life and death which possess the same character and with which the eucharist is indissolubly linked? Is the search for a fully satisfactory use of this language any more hopeful now that we are better placed to look at it as language, that is, as a tool for our use, and now that we are more coolly aware of its pedigree; or is this path too overgrown for further progress to be profitable, so that the best thing is to abandon it altogether and look for other terms?

One of the difficulties with most of the commonest formulations involving sacrificial language is that they start too far up the conceptual ladder; that is, they presuppose more fundamental theological concepts which seem not to be fully clear, like a mountain whose summit is exposed while the lower levels are shrouded in mist. This is what we meant when we said earlier that these lines of thought fail to do justice to doctrine on which they rest. Consider statements like 'we offer Christ in the eucharist'; 'Christ pleads his sacrifice in the eucharist'; 'we unite our offering with Christ's oblation on Calvary'. These and others are all hard to expound satisfactorily once they are explored in the context of basic Christian belief (for example, about our relationship to Christ and the effect of his life and death).

They also fail another test. All of them unashamedly mix two levels of discourse and speak in one breath of heavenly 'events' and earthly actions. It may be a better procedure to start from the latter, and to give a clear account of the eucharist at that level, before going on to say what the rite signifies in terms of our understanding of God. The eucharist *is*, then, as an earthly action, a blessing and sharing of bread and wine by Christian believers, on the warrant of the Last Supper. What can this act fittingly say about God, in the light of our whole awareness of him? This is the question to ask.

In all this discussion there is one assumption which at this point needs to be brought to the surface: that the eucharist is to be seen as the act which sums up and expresses the whole Christian faith, the act which stands at the hub of Christian life – as it were, the tribal dance of the Christians, embodying and strengthening the world-outlook which binds them together. It is only if this view is held that the attempt to see it in the setting of the whole structure of Christian doctrine will arise and be taken seriously as a theological task. If on the contrary the eucharist is taken to be simply one item in Christian life alongside others, belief about it may well be regarded as a relatively autonomous subject. The validity of various ways of speaking of it will tend to be judged not by rigorous standards of consistency and coherence but rather by the different and perhaps more subjective standards of devotional suitability. The lack of conceptual interconnectedness between different ideas will be no bar to their value or to their claim to a place in Christian use. Those who see the eucharist simply as one among a number of God's gracious provisions for his people will tend to opt for this second view. Those who see it as much more central than that cannot avoid facing the fundamental questions which we have been asking.

If we take this more comprehensive approach, remembering our concern with sacrifice, we might have before us this statement of Augustine: 'A true sacrifice is any act that is done in order that we may cleave in holy union to God.' On this broad definition, the eucharist surely has a character which can be appropriately spoken of as sacrificial; but if this is more than incidental, it must be more integrally related to its specific features than a phrase like, for example, 'sacrifice of praise' implies. The general idea of the eucharist as a Godward act needs to be developed with reference to the character of the rite itself.

In other words, if eucharistic doctrine is to be satisfactory, it needs to take seriously two starting-points: the nature and will of God for us, and the character of the rite. As it is God's revealed nature to give himself with a completeness of which Calvary is the measure, and his will that we should give ourselves wholly to him, the eucharist, if it is to embody this faith, must make its expression possible. At two levels, the rite does precisely this. First, at the natural level, its framing in a shared meal brings to

bear all the implications of common belief, aspiration and purpose. Second, at the level of what is almost tautology, the solemn
blessing of the bread and wine serves to designate them for the
very purpose of expressing what the rite is concerned to accomplish. From one point of view it 'works' at the level of psychology,
for it 'conditions' the Christians to hold more firmly and to be
more identified with the faith which they bring to it.[7] The tribal
dance binds together the tribe. It is nevertheless the 'act' of God,
through the accredited means, for it is, we believe, his will to
accomplish this purpose in his people by this rite. The action of
thanksgiving-cum-communion matches the purpose which it
serves.

   Finally, however rigidly and mistakenly the relationship of
Christ's self-offering and the eucharist has often been expressed,
the instinct which pressed towards identifying them was not
fundamentally at fault. For wherever God acts in the cause of
bringing men to true relationship with himself, he acts unre-
servedly as himself and exhibits always the same dependable
characteristics; whether in the person of Jesus or in the sacrament
of the eucharist or in any facet of the work of his grace. It is a pity
that the road by which the term 'sacrifice' first entered the discussion and then subsequently developed was such as to render
the proper use of this most striking image highly problematical.
Over the centuries, the language of eucharistic sacrifice has
turned into a minefield in which it has been hard to tread with
safety, though many have shown a remarkable capacity for refus-
ing to disintegrate even when they have been blown up. But
through all vicissitudes of theology, the eucharist remains the
outstanding means by which God's people bring to a focus their
total corporate and individual self-offering to him, because of
Jesus, who both showed us the way and gave us the rite by which
to grow in it. God's gift 'in Christ' and our response 'in Christ'
meet and fuse in the single act.

## Notes

   1. The writer was much helped by reflections offered by the Revd
Canon E. B. M. Green.
   2. Cf. M. F. Wiles, *The Making of Christian Doctrine*, Cambridge University Press 1967, pp.121f.
   3. Cf. E. C. Ratcliff and A. H. Couratin, 'The Early Roman Canon
Missae', *Journal of Ecclesiastical History* XX, 1969, pp.211ff.

4. See Francis Clark, *Eucharistic Sacrifice and the Reformation*, Darton Longman & Todd 1960, Newman Press 1961, pp.169ff.

5. See P. E. More and F. L. Cross (eds.), *Anglicanism*, SPCK 1951, pp.495f., for examples from the seventeenth century.

6. See E. L. Mascall, *Corpus Christi*, Longmans 1953.

7. See James Lambert, *Science and Sanctity*, Faith Press 1961, pp.44ff.

# 7

# *Liturgy and her Companions: A Theological Appraisal*

Among the learned and informative essays that make up this book,* this one is an oddity, for it neither displays learning nor conveys information. It is an infernal cheek for it to be offered at all. And besides the oddness, there are two other charges against it. First, its tone is generally detached and may strike some readers as aloof. Look at it another way, however, and that may be no bad thing. There is something to be said for standing back from the task of making liturgy and, however sketchily, assessing where it has got to in the setting of the wider theological enterprise.

Second, this article comes from a member of the Liturgical Commission of the Church of England. He is therefore one of the sponsors of the Series 3 eucharistic rite. Then how dare he remove himself from the font and point a critical finger at the tender infant at the solemn moment of its entry into the life of the church? His answer is that sponsorship can be of two kinds. There is acceptance in a practical spirit of the best that can be achieved in the circumstances. Liturgical commissions do not operate in the best of all possible worlds and they are probably not the best possible tool for carrying out the work assigned to them; they work within the circumstances provided for them and they do their best. There is also the enthusiastic welcoming of a superlatively excellent creation. I doubt whether the approval felt by any members of the Commission is quite of this character, though some may go varying distances beyond the sober commendation I mentioned first. On the whole, I cannot, partly for reasons far beyond the control of the Commission; and this essay helps to show why.

*The Eucharist Today*, ed. R. C. D. Jasper, SPCK 1974.

They do their best in the circumstances, I say. Those circumstances (the procedures laid down, certain directions dictated by pastoral necessity) may seem pretty strange when regarded from the point of view of this essay, for my aim is to see what the recent developments look like from the side of current theology as a whole. From other points of view, they may be wholly understandable, inevitable, and even laudable. But from the point of view of a concern with pure Christian truth (a luxury at the best of times), they are strange.

Liturgy, I take it, is the expression of the faith of Christians in word and action, appropriate in a given situation, for the purpose of the worship of God. In a sense, therefore, it should spring from the participants themselves; and such informal making of liturgy is likely to become commoner, for good or ill, even in the traditionally 'fixed form' churches. But in practice, clearly, churches must and will continue to compose and authorize liturgies formally and centrally. For in liturgy, Christians must seek to avoid the risk of simply 'expressing *themselves*': they must express not only the faith they have grasped but the faith which has grasped them. One of liturgy's roles is to draw Christians towards a spirituality and an understanding of God better than that which they usually reach.

Churches have taken to composing liturgies by a mixed procedure which, whatever its virtues, is certainly calculated to extinguish any chance of the second kind of approval I referred to. Expert committees and synods, taking their various parts, may arrive at a workable consensus. They will scarcely produce a masterpiece to warm the heart and catch the imagination.

But our concern is with theology. We turn then to inquire into the bases on which liturgy is nowadays constructed. The two dominant foundations are current practice and liturgical principles. The first is a matter of pastoral politics. Not all churchgoers revel in novelty! New liturgy must start from old liturgy, contain a few familiar landmarks, and develop step by step. In due course, language may be modernized and old forms quietly dropped in favour of new ones. But, however delicate pastorally, all this is, from the theological point of view, relatively simple. It may take time, it will meet resistance, it is hard to write good new words or decide on suitable criteria for 'modern liturgical English', but conceptually there is no great complexity. It is when we come to the second matter, liturgical principles, that we must dig deeper.

Let me come out with it straight away. If you do dig, you find an astonishing phenomenon. You discover that the principles of liturgy have become a discipline in their own right, quite apart from other aspects of Christian thought. It is a fact that is worth contemplating, for it is surely quite new in Christian life, that liturgy can be constructed without significant reference to the total theological scene and seeing itself as an independent skill. Is this not disturbing?

It is of course a result of the increasing specialization of scholarship. If the expert student of the Old Testament finds it harder and harder to talk professionally to the student of doctrine, why should the student of liturgy be less expert and therefore less segregated? Let the army of the liturgists arise and assert their legitimate independence and integrity. The march of knowledge is such that they can hardly do otherwise. And why should not the church pay heed to them in their own sphere, as it listens to the architects in theirs and (ah! hopefully) to the theologians in theirs? They are the experts, they know the rules of their own discipline: they should be heard, and, with due attention to what pew-sitting Jones will swallow, followed.

But even from the purely academic point of view, specialization is not all gain. The specialist needs to give way to, or at least co-operate with, the interdisciplinary man, if his subject is not to lack a sense of its true context and turn into a private world. And when the speciality finds application in life, talk across the boundaries is imperative.

Liturgical studies have made immense strides in the last hundred years, and, as in other branches of theology, most of the work has been historical in character. The story of the development of the church's worship has been to a large degree uncovered and plotted. As a result, the principles on which the liturgies of the past were formed are clear to us. We know their shape, their structure, and their stories, and we understand the contexts in which they arose. Amid the detail and the variety, we can broadly generalize. We can say what the shape of the eucharistic liturgy *is* – or, more accurately, has been. And there's one of the rubs. How far is the past determinative for the present? In recent liturgy-making, throughout Christendom, it has become more, not less, so. Modernizing of liturgy has meant certainly a new clothing of language, but the old lady who wears it would in her inmost heart be more at home with Hippolytus than with Cranmer or Bucer, let alone the hippy liturgists of whom she has, she is relieved to say, scarcely heard.

If it was only a matter of structure, there might be little reason for complaint. There are clearly good working grounds for knowing fairly clearly what a eucharist 'is', and the traditional structure, now revived, will, in that sense, do very nicely for most purposes, though we may resist too absolute an advocacy in its favour.

So far the liturgists may well have their head. But liturgy-making cannot properly go further as an independent craft; its task is to provide the forms by which Christians express their faith in corporate worship. It is bound to look across the frontiers into the lands of biblical studies and doctrine as they stand at the present day. Its task is not simply to update or revive the liturgies of the past, but to reflect the best understanding of God in the church of the present.

Nor does it stop there. For Christians do not, we hope, respond to God, or think about him, wearing wholly exotic clothes. They do it as men of their time, with certain angles of vision and certain ideas inevitably before them. The present-day Christian will then surely wish, as he approaches the task of thinking about his worship, to use the insights of anthropology, psychology, and sociology which bear upon it – not in order to 'secularize' or 'de-Christianize' his work, but in order to undertake it with his mind alert to everything that concerns it.

It is no exaggeration to say that modern liturgy-making has scarcely glanced into any of these territories. 'Liturgical principles' have hardly begun to rub up against 'biblical principles' or 'doctrinal principles', let alone considerations arising from more basic fields of study. When they do, the sparks tend to fly; or else, sadly, the two pieces of machinery have no capacity to interact. But if the sparks could fly, then the resulting blaze might purify as well as consume. It would be justified if the resulting liturgy said what was in the widest way 'real' for the faith of those who used it and was no longer the expression of venerable but now alien ideas. Again, this is not an appeal for 'modern thought' to be the arbiter of Christian thought and speech. It is an appeal for recognition of the fact that Christian thought as well as Christian language can become archaic, and may go on being expressed even when it has no compensating quality (for example, its evocative power) to commend it. There is no call to deny that on grounds which are an indefinable amalgam of spirituality and aesthetics, there is good reason to keep, for certain purposes, old liturgies: but our concern here is with the new.

Let us look at a few symptoms. Liturgical principle dictates that the thanksgiving in the eucharist should be prefaced by a thankful rehearsal of the 'acts' of God for man's salvation. No proposal could be more apt and even if it springs from age-long tradition it is not necessarily any the worse for that. But perhaps it would not be amiss if the way in which those 'acts' were rehearsed received a new look, in the light of what we really believe. Few would surely contest my right to put the word 'acts' in quotation marks, however shadowy, for actions by God are not quite as actions by men. The analogy is imperfect, and that which tends to receive this description may often be better spoken of in other terms. The use of the analogy may lead theological truth to be stated in a mythological idiom, which was once virtually unchallenged and which now easily deflects attention from the truth itself instead of aiding its comprehension. Demythologizing, whether mild or severe, may indeed lead to an impoverishment of imagery. It can equally lead to a restoration of a sense of the living God by removing the opiate of an obsolete story.

The Series 3 prayer will give us an illustration. Like its Series 2 predecessor and the ancient models, it speaks entirely in its preface of alleged 'events' of the distant past, while admittedly drawing some attention to their lasting effect. God, ages ago, created, gave liberation from sin, and brought into being a people for his own possession. But few really believe that creation is something which God *did* in some immeasurably deep past, and if they do believe that, then their faith in God the Creator is severely deficient. If Christians are thought to believe it, then, in the eyes of others who may be initially disposed towards Christianity, so much the worse for them. And however much weight we place on the life and death of Jesus, the faithful believer will not be content to see 'redemption' as tied exclusively to those events; it is something which he knows here and now in his present relationship with God, and to speak of it solely in past terms is to remove that vital dimension. 'Creation' and 'redemption' may speak of the past, but they speak at least equally of the setting in which we now live. Is not the recognition of this the distinctive fact about Christian existence which we meet to celebrate in the eucharist? We live now in the gracious hand of God.

Yet though the Christian knows this and lives by it, liturgy fails to reflect it. The old purely historical-cum-mythological approach persists – in obedience to liturgical tradition, and, behind that, to a canonizing of a particular way of regarding the witness of scripture.

What then of the Bible in relation to modern liturgy-making? In the Roman communion in particular – and it has reverberated among us all – the liturgical and biblical revivals have gone hand in hand. When it comes to the practical effect of their collaboration in the composition of liturgies, it can scarcely be maintained that the full resources of modern biblical scholarship have been taken into account. Rather, it seems to be deemed sufficient to make liturgical forms virtually catenae of biblical words and images. To do that is to 'use' the Bible. There has been little sign of any serious attempt to consider whether these words and images still carry their former vividness or are intelligible expressions of what is to be said. Nor is there much sign of awareness of the echoes and contexts of biblical allusions: the mere fact of allusion is sufficient.

For example, again in the thanksgiving, again with ample precedent, we praise God for creation through Jesus, his living Word. We appeal thereby to a biblical and patristic concept, that of Christ as the pre-existent Logos, which is more remote from present-day thought than almost any other and which is so far removed from readily accessible imagery that its evocative power is minimal, except for the initiated. Hardly one worshipper in thousands can be expected to find it an appropriate expression of his faith.

But quite apart from cases of extreme difficulty such as this, which arise from a too determined and unsubtle biblicism, is continual biblical allusion necessarily the right way to make satisfactory modern liturgy? May twentieth-century Christians not pray in words of their own, for their own intrinsic power – including their power to evoke significant reflection – or must we be afraid that unless we cling to the mere letter of scripture the spirit of the age will banish authentic Christian truth? Yet we hardly safeguard Christian truth merely by uttering its old words, out of context and unexplained. There has been little attempt to make sure they are used in such a way as to draw out their genuine power in a modern setting.

The main achievements of modern liturgy-making have been these: to make plain the structure of the eucharist in a way that is clear-cut as well as traditional; to modernize the language to some degree – though with haziness about criteria; and to make it easier for the rite to be seen as the common act of the Christian community.

But despite the widespread feeling that enough is enough where liturgical reform is concerned, it would be a grave mistake to suppose that a satisfactory terminus has now been reached. Many will complain that the Series 3 service is too 'modern'; but from some points of view – and they might be shared by many of the complainers if they were really to search their hearts – it is archaic. Its thought forms and theological assumptions are wholly traditional. Apart from a few traces of Reformation emphases (more now than in Series 2), there is little sign of any development in Christian theology since patristic times, let alone in the last hundred years. Yet in that period both the achievements of, and challenges to, Christian thought have been, to say the least, substantial. That they find no echo in the words thought suitable for Christian worship may reflect an existing state of affairs – the virtual isolation of the great majority of believers from both the achievements and the challenges. That in itself is a matter worth pondering. But one role of liturgy is to reflect not just what the church *is*, but what it should be. And should the church, even when it gathers for its most domestic acts (which are also the most universal in scope), not aim to be aware of its position in the world and of the needs of Christian statement in the world which the worshippers in fact inhabit and in which their witness is made? It is true of course that statement in worship demands a different range of considerations from statement in theological discussion. But the difference between the two modes should be one consciously arrived at in the full light of the needs and contributions of both. In fact it exists because the two have not yet troubled to get on to speaking terms.

Nobody wants a liturgical idiom which is aridly precise in its conceptual clarity. Let the imagery be as riotous and exciting as possible. At present we fail to do justice either to the needs which such a policy might serve or to the legitimate questions of the theologian and the worshipper who notices the words he is required to use. (It is too rarely recognized how close the questions of the theologian are to those of the 'ordinary man' when he gives his mind to what he really finds thinkable.)

In my examples, I have confined myself to major matters – the doctrine of God and the use of the Bible. Others are subordinate and have received more attention in the discussion aroused by the publication of the new service. But features like the heavy emphasis on penitence and the inclusion of the (albeit optional) decalogue are not wholly untypical of the approaches we have had in mind.

A priest once observed in a television programme, speaking of the liturgical needs of his people, that theology and history are 'a luxury for eggheads' and that what people need is to catch the mystery of God. If that were all the truth, rites would be a matter of indifference, and we should certainly do better simply to hold on to our old forms; partly because old words are one of the best devices for aiding the sense of mystery and partly because the enterprise of reform would not be worth the trouble. But Christian worship is not simply a channel of religious feeling or an inroad to the mystery of God. It is an approach by thinking men to a God about whom beliefs are held and who has made it possible for men to speak about him in intelligible terms. Rite is then not a matter of indifference; and the mere continuance of old forms, defensible though it is, ought not to claim a monopoly. But if we are to modernize, then in the long run the process must be thoroughgoing. It cannot properly be limited to certain aspects of the matter. Liturgists as such have now perhaps done all they can, given the conventions in which their discipline has come to work. Either they must widen their horizon or they must enlist men of other crafts, both within the traditional frontiers of theological study and outside them, if God's people are to be able to express themselves wholeheartedly in worship. If they fail to do this, it will not be surprising that many will continue to find old ways better, for in certain respects they had the capacity to evoke men's deepest Christian feelings and were so blatantly ancient that the worshipper made allowances which in using modern liturgies he may not expect to make. The fact is that liturgy gathers to itself many more considerations than the study of liturgy, as an academic discipline, or liturgical reform, as an ecclesiastical occupation, or for that matter theology in its widest sense, tend to reckon with. The worship of God needs to enlist them all.

# 8

## *Priesthood*

This paper does not aim to give a comprehensive account of the theological issues included in its subject, nor does it attempt a neutral dispassionate survey of those topics which have been selected for treatment. Rather, by taking its own positive way and departing from customary idiom, it seeks to stimulate and forward discussion of priesthood.

We must begin by defining our subject, for the term priesthood is not free from ambiguities. It may refer simply to the second order of ministry in the traditional scheme, those clergy who are neither bishops nor deacons. Here we wish to use it more generally than that, to denote the normal, central exercise of ministry in the church, wherever it is found and in whatever way it is arranged. Some will prefer not to use this word for this purpose, and we shall attempt to meet some of their objections (though sometimes obliquely) in the course of this essay. In using the word as widely as this, we include, alongside those who technically bear the name of priests, all (such as bishops and non-episcopal ministers) who carry out that amalgam of worshipping, preaching, teaching, and caring which makes up the normal work of the Christian clergy. The fact that there are some in holy orders whose work does not chiefly fall under these headings at first sight creates an anomaly: to them we shall return in due course. We start from what remains the normal area of activity of the vast majority of Christian clergy.

But the term priesthood is not the only one to yield this area of meaning. Ministry or clergy would do almost as well for precisely the same purpose, though neither of them is easily confined to those we have in mind. But priesthood is our subject, and if we are to use it in the general sense just suggested, we must note its special flavour and associations. At the outset, discussion is bedevilled by a mistake and a confusion, both of them responsible for theological difficulty which is at least partly unnecessary.

We look first at the mistake, which results from a piece of imperfect typology. In the early church, and in the church in North Africa particularly, one way of relating the old covenant to the new was by way of a simple parallelism of ingredients. The arrangements and institutions of the old religion of Israel demonstrated what was, so to speak, the right equipment which authentic religion ought to possess; the arrangements of the church could be expected to display the same features, albeit in a new form. Thus, baptism corresponded to circumcision, Sunday to Sabbath, eucharist to the old sacrifices, and Christian priesthood to Aaronic. Clearly, such a procedure may be edifying and instructive, but it can also lead into dangerous paths when used as a basis for theology. Above all, the role of Christ in this pattern is too incidental. As far as the actual structure of the pattern is concerned, he is simply the agent who ends the old regime and begins the new; but he is hardly the key point in any more organic sense than this.

In true typology, on the other hand, Christ is the control; by reference to his life, death, and resurrection alone can it be determined which Old Testament themes and images are appropriate to illuminate him and which are to emerge for transformed service in the thought and language of the church. The old images all come to meet in him; the new all spring from him. The unsuitable ones are discarded, and none has any validity which is independent of him.

Much of the unease at the term priesthood comes from its use in theological statement which belongs to imperfect typology. This is at work when the priest is seen as the one whose chief task (the one that gives him this title) is to offer the eucharist, the sacrifice of the new covenant, just as Aaronic priests offered the sacrifices of the old. Such statement may or may not be appropriate, but whether it is or not depends solely upon its coherence with true typology (that is, valid use of the term priesthood to describe the clergy must be derived from the theology of the person and work of Christ and not on a pattern based on mere parallelism, however neat and attractive). So much for the mistake.

The confusion results from over-devotion to the letter of New Testament texts as raw materials for theological statement. It is true that in the New Testament the term priest is hardly applied to anyone who could conceivably be thought of as a clergyman (the nearest is St Paul in a fleeting metaphor in Rom. 15.16 and

Phil. 2.17). It is applied to Christ (Heb. 5.1-10; 8.1f.; John 17). It is applied perhaps to God (Rom. 3.25), and certainly to the Christian people, both in the present (I Peter 2.5-9) and in the future (Rev. 5.10; 20.6). The temptation is to suppose first that Christians ought never to use the term except in one of these senses, and secondly that these varied uses ought somehow to be capable of being related to one another *in terms of the word priest*.[1] In truth there is no problem here, at least not in this form. It is a matter of the same image or concept being used by independent writers in a variety of ways for a number of different purposes for which it seemed to them appropriate. This is a perfectly understandable procedure which contains no mystery and does not call for the harmonizing of the different applications. Nor does it carry with it a demand that the term should not be applied to the clergy if the image is in some way appropriate to describe their function. To apply it to the clergy in this way implies no disparagement of the Christian people as a whole: it can be applied to them to make equally valid but different points. It is a matter of defining the precise function of the image in each particular case. Certainly, when the writer of I Peter applies the term to the whole Christian people, he is not attributing some sort of clerical status to all Christians in any modern sense, nor is he affirming that clerical office is to be excluded or lightly esteemed by Christian theology; he is not raising issues of this kind at all. Similarly, when the work of Christ is described in priestly terms in the epistle to the Hebrews, nothing is being either affirmed or denied about Christian clergy; the matter is not in mind. The most that can be said is that the uses of this image of priesthood in the New Testament may contribute to the building up of a theological framework which excludes certain views of the status and role of the clergy; but this is nothing to do with the term priest itself – it is a matter of a whole pattern of doctrine.

Though the mistake and the confusion to which we have referred have caused much gratuitous difficulty in discussion of this matter, real issues lie behind them – often less to do with priesthood itself than with other, more central doctrinal matters such as the work of Christ and the believer's relationship with him. As we turn now to make a constructive statement of the theology of priesthood, these matters will be continually in mind, and we shall endeavour to do them justice as far as the scope of the discussion permits.

.   .   .

We must state our principles. First, nothing whatsoever impairs the uniqueness of Christ as the bearer of God to man and as the means of man's return to God. The uniqueness consists in the totality of his giving of himself to the Father for these ends, and in the divine place which he occupies in God's action towards man for their accomplishment. It clearly does not imply that others do not also perform these tasks *in their own proper manner and degree.* Holy men of all kinds, whether Christian or not, participate in the work of bearing God to man and enabling man to return to God. We therefore relate the activity of these men to that of Christ by speaking of it as a participation in his unique mediatorial role. Whether they do it consciously or not, all such men share in the divine purpose which Christ embodies, but they do it wholly by dependence upon him. By baptism all Christians are potentially of this company because they are in the sphere where the articulate word of the gospel is heard, and so can bring to bear upon others the work of Christ with all fullness and clarity. Whatever is to be said about the clergy's particular role, it must be consistent with this.

Secondly, nothing whatever impairs the equality of all Christians in their direct relationship with God and in their enjoyment of the benefits of Christ's work. But equality in these crucial respects leaves entirely open the possibility of inequality in other respects, and makes it neither more nor less likely that such inequality is consistent with God's purposes. It is clear, for example, that several New Testament writers were far from extending the equality of all Christians to the exercise of functions in the church. St Paul welcomed the fact that a wide variety of charismata was bestowed upon the members of a relatively small congregation (I Cor. 12), and saw in this nothing incompatible with their equal participation in the Christian status. Whether a particular Christian group puts more stress on the respects in which Christians are equal or the respects in which they are unequal depends commonly upon factors which are only loosely related to Christian theology. Thus, excessively rigid hierarchy or the disesteeming of some parts of the Christian community and the exalting of others (usually the laity and the clergy respectively!) result from political, economic, and social pressures which are not difficult to identify. In such circumstances, theological argument tends to limp behind the situation it must somehow justify. Similarly, the strong and overriding assertion of the equality of all Christians is often more a reaction against over-rigid hierarchy than a really valid generalization from those respects in which it is undoubtedly justified.

The third principle is connected with the fact that differentiation of function within the Christian community does not in itself impair Christian equality, and leads us to the reason why this is so. We propose to give full value to the fact that God's work is thoroughly sacramental in character. With Christ himself as the supreme instance, God communicates himself to man through people, things, and acts. Even abstract ideas are always indissoluble from the personalities and circumstances of those who formulate and utter them. The word is always made flesh. The people, things, and acts which are God's sacramental agents come to man intimately, intensively, and radically, if he allows them to do so, and affect his whole person and life. Those rites which the church names technically as sacraments are of course central examples of this. Too often, because they seem small in their effects by comparison with the great power inherent in them, they are expounded in terms other than these. Either they are made to depend for their reality upon human response, and so their standing as acts of God is neglected, or they are accorded a rather harsh, impersonal objectivity in the attempt to make them as independent as possible of the response given to them. But God's action is nothing if not personal in its character; what he proffers to man, in sacraments as in all his other actions, is his whole self, seeking union with each human creature. His action always, then, aims at the most profound effects upon man and means to achieve them in the end. It goes without saying that the personal character of God's action means that it is never a matter of generality but always of particularity. It is the same eucharist which feeds all God's people, but what God designs to accomplish by it in the life of each is entirely moulded to the needs of each. It follows that in a world created and indwelt by God it is important never to undervalue theologically, never to minimize divine significance in rites and institutions where it ought to be maximized. Wherever God acts, he acts fully.

Priesthood is to be understood in the light of these considerations. This is so first in relation to the functions which the clergy perform in the setting of the whole church. Continually, they act as sacramental persons, instruments of God's purposes in a wide variety of ways. However 'low' a doctrine of the ministry a Christian group may have, it cannot prevent such officers as it possesses acquiring a representative character, and this inevitably shapes the character of their work. They act not only in their individual capacities, with their personal talents and defects, but as standing for God in the Christian community. To that degree and in that sense their action always has an impersonal aspect. But in the sense that it is always the action of one man towards others, their work is always intensely personal – and so the appropriate means of God's personal action towards us. Of course, on this second side, the bearer of priesthood cannot be distinguished in certain ways from any other Christian; but his representative capacity does give him a special place. We must not accord this a merely incidental significance; the differences of function within the church are themselves means of grace (charismata) and not just convenient ways of getting some of the church's work done (that is, they convey to the Christian community, in visible personal form, various facets of the divine work and character). This is the proper function of hierarchy in the church, and as long as it acts in this way, it does nothing to spoil but rather enhances the essential equalities of the whole Christian people. When it fails to act thus, the results can of course be disastrous in that the structure of the church's leadership turns out to belie the gospel it preaches. Thus a tyrant-bishop may well give to his subordinates many unsought opportunities for spiritual advancement through mortification of their wills, but he hardly serves to stimulate life-giving charity among his people.

The sacramental character of God's work points the way not only to the understanding of the work of priesthood, but also to the evaluation of those who bear it. In the first place, it explains why the name of priest should be a suitable one for the Christian clergy, why (to revert to our earlier remarks) this image should be appropriately applied in Christian usage to a body of men for whom the New Testament did not use it and to whom it was originally applied by a piece of imperfect typologizing. The image or idea of priesthood, especially in the biblical tradition, brings together a number of concepts: in particular, representation, mediation, sacrifice, and leadership of others into access to God. All these ideas apply in one way or another to the actual role of the Christian clergy. As we have seen, in whatever Christian group they exist, their representative function is inescapable, however strenuously the doctrinal implications of it are restricted. Inevitably too, the clergy's work involves acting as agents for transmitting the things of God to men, in particular the gospel and the sacraments, but also the pastoral care which the church exercises as the instrument of the Good Shepherd. There is room for difference of opinion how far these tasks, undeniably associated with the clergy, should be confined to them. Some tasks, such as the pastoral, are not necessarily theirs alone, and it is worth asking whether there is any substantial theological reason why others (such as presiding at the eucharist) should not similarly be regarded as only conventionally their sole province. To answer this, let us look more closely at the instance we have mentioned, the pastoral office. While no one would claim that this should be confined to the clergy, for it is clearly one aspect of the charity required of all Christians, it remains true that in actual fact it is most intensively exercised over the whole range of the Christian community by the clergy alone. Where others share in it, it is usually with regard to a few specific individuals (family or friends), or, in the case of those whose profession is pastoral in nature (for example, teachers or nurses) with regard to one single category of persons (the young or the sick). In practice, then, the pastoral task is normally carried out, in the setting of the entire Christian community, by the clergy. And in a world sacramentally worked upon by God practice is far from incidental to theological statement. The practice is part of the empirical base for the action of God through priesthood and therefore for its theological significance in the whole work of God towards man.

The sacrificial associations of priesthood are equally important in that the clergy are called upon to bear the marks of that self-giving love which Christ shows to be the overriding characteristic of God. Again, this is something they share with all Christians, but still they exercise this role with special prominence. Once more, the practicalities are to be used theologically, for it is certainly the case that the sacrificial self-giving of the clergy, in prayer and in virtue, is the stimulus and encouragement from which others profit, and its lack is a scandal which frustrates the rest. In this respect as in others, the bearer of priesthood is the sacramental agent of God's own love centrally embodied in Christ.

Priesthood is associated with the leading of others into closer access to God. This was the aspect of priesthood upon which the author of Hebrews seized when he applied the image to the work of Christ. In their own different way, in strict dependence upon Christ and their life in him, the clergy share this characteristic. In their case it depends partly on their performance of certain acts where their personalities count for little (baptizing, reading services), partly on their holiness of life, and partly on their technical expertise. Not all these features will be present in all clergy in substantial degree, but certainly they all belong to the function of priesthood. The last of the three is worth special note because it is often treated as if it were incidental to the essence of the matter. If it is left out of account, it becomes easier to treat the work of priesthood as a series of tasks, some apparently requiring little skill, which are allocated to certain persons in the church by way of sheer convenience or order. This tendency in much modern discussion sees ordination as no more than an authorization by the church, which forms, so to speak, only an outer skin upon its bearer. We shall see other reasons for being unwilling to accept this view, but one reason is certainly the existence of the technical skills, going to the roots of a man's being and attitudes, which the priest needs to possess. These are not simply the skills which a lay theologian equally possesses (for example, in biblical study, doctrine, or church history), but arise from the theological formation demanded by the specific work of priesthood. They are stimulated by, and directed towards, that work, and therefore include (for example) extra attention to ascetic and moral theology. Moreover all theology will be studied in the context of the needs of the work and so will have a pastoral and apologetic slant. The technical skills which the priest acquires over the years by a mixture of study and experience are another part of the data through which God uses these persons sacramentally, to be the agents of his work. Their theological significance is, in the world of a God who acts sacramentally, indissolubly bound up with their actual work and activity.

The sacramental approach to God's work also helps to evaluate the theological significance of priesthood, in that it draws attention to the extent of the divine action within the priest himself. God forms a man in his whole personality for perfect relationship with himself, and in so doing deals with him in his whole setting in life. The work which a man undertakes and the skills which he acquires are a most important part of that setting, and, far from being a superficial layer on top of his 'real personality', are wholly integrated with him. It is a question of the relation of function to person. Christianly speaking, we are, presumably, never happy with a total divorce between the two though for certain purposes we are ready to tolerate it. When we have to buy groceries, we bear with the fact the grocer is uncharitable or adulterous provided that he manages his business efficiently; pastorally speaking, in relation to him as a whole person, we are concerned to remedy the situation. In the case of a Christian, we desire that moral conduct should match the performance of outward Christian duties, and we look for such an integrity of person that it is meaningless to ask when he is acting as a Christian and when he is being himself.

In the case of the priesthood, nobody wants totally to divorce function from person, though some lines of discussion come perilously near it; quite often there is found an unwillingness to admit that anything is demanded of a clergyman, apart from function, that is not demanded equally of any other Christian. This undervalues the importance of function in relation to personality. Because the function differs, the demand also differs. The priest is to be a priest, whole and integrated, not a layman doing priestly tasks. The priesthood is to take hold of his whole personality, so that he lives what he is. It should be meaningless to ask of any of his significant thoughts or actions whether he is acting as a priest or as himself. The traditional notion of indelible character, juridical though it may be in some formulations (necessary perhaps to deal with hard cases), may usefully be considered along these lines. If a man becomes *this* kind of man with integrity, he cannot cease to be what he is.

Of course the same may be true of a Christian teacher or a Christian bricklayer. Only for certain purposes (the professional or the liturgical) is the division simply into clergy and laity, as the two categories comprising the church, the meaningful one. For many purposes, we need to make many more divisions, as St Paul did. The Christian teacher will acquire one kind of integrated Christian being, resulting from the operation of grace upon his own personality and the needs of his calling, and the Christian bricklayer another. Yet nobody has ever claimed to ordain a man for life to Christian bricklayership, though if one may interpret the Pauline lists so, it may be that they once did see people as ordained to Christian teacherhood, and when a nun is professed in a teaching order, it is not very different from it. We do, however, make much more of ordaining clergy to permanent status; and this is wholly justifiable within the context of the church as the microcosmic, pioneer community within mankind. For while the church could survive (and almost does!) without Christian bricklayers and even without Christian teachers, it could not reasonably survive without priests. These particular people whose functions are indissoluble from their personality are essential to the church: not just juridically, in that it has been laid down, for example, that the eucharist can be celebrated only by a bishop or a priest, but much more fundamentally, in that God can only mediate himself to man by means of other men, and the church needs to externalize and focus certain necessary functions upon particular persons. Some of them can be done by others fragmentarily (for example, the pastoral function), but they need to find focal and central expression in those who will *be*, exist as, pastors (or whatever function one has in mind). Walking men need walking sacraments. As in marriage a man in relation to his wife experiences, and does not just think about, the love of Christ and his church, so in relation to the priest a man experiences, and does not just think about, the divine fatherhood or the divine forgiveness; and this is appropriate to our human condition. Such a provision is of a piece with the nature of a Creator God and a God who incarnates himself within the creation.

This approach to the theology of priesthood has been concerned chiefly with the place of the clergy in the church, but the same considerations can easily be extended to their work as representatives of Christ and his church to those outside. Here again, the priest acts on behalf of Christ expressed in the Christian community, bearing his charity or the explicit word of the gospel, as appropriate to the needs of those with whom he deals. In no case does he act as a solitary, simply on his own private credentials, but always as a sacrament of him whom he serves.

Because we have concentrated on the place of the clergy in the church, we have also neglected all exercises of priesthood apart from the most central and normal: the priest in relation to a fairly static Christian group. There have long been many (priest-monks, schoolmasters in holy orders) who have been 'off-centre' from this point of view. It is likely that at least in highly mobile Western society their number and variety will increase; the priest-worker, the chaplain to a single social group, the priest-religious – these are likely to be more and more in demand as agents of pastoral care and evangelism, or simply of Christian presence. But just as bad or unskilled priests do not affect the fact that the norm is a virtuous and competent priest, so such ways of exercising priesthood do not affect the fact that the normal place for the priest, theologically and in practice, is at the heart of the Christian community, which has the eucharist for its typical manifestation of itself. This is where, as a sacramental person, he chiefly belongs; and the test of whether men acting outside this setting should be ordained or not will lie in the degree to which their roles seem to be reasonable deviations from the norm and retain enough of its features.

Because the priest is a sacramental person whose whole being is to be penetrated by God for the purposes of his calling, his ordinary humanity may seem in danger of being obliterated, as if ordination brought him into a caste apart. But this is not so, except in the sense that the particularity of each man makes him in God's eyes a caste of one! Rather, a man's ordinary humanity is enhanced by his discovering the role in which he is to grow towards God, and the priesthood is no exception. Renunciations which the priest may be called upon to make (for example, marriage or wealth, in certain cases) are no monopoly of his among the servants of God.

There are many other questions concerning priesthood, some of great importance, to which we have not even referred; but the approach we have adopted may point to a line of treatment for some of them. We have spoken of the thorough involvement of God in the rites and institutions which he gives to us and of maximizing their theological value (that is, seeing them fully as his acts). It seems to be consistent with this that the historical continuity of priesthood is a factor of importance, though only one element among others in assessing its value. How exactly it should be related to particular historical manifestations of priesthood is outside our scope. Whether it is consistent with this approach that women should be ordained is another topic which we do not propose to discuss, but certainly the question ought to be tackled in these terms. The psychological and social practicalities involved are not to be seen as factors which prevent clear abstract theology having free course, but are part of the data for making the theology.

It is often disputed whether the ministry is theologically prior to the church or dependent upon it, whether its authority is from above or from below. It ought be to be clear that we should refuse to choose between such falsely posed alternatives. The church simply exists, by God's disposition, in differentiated form: there are many gifts but one Spirit. Of course, therefore, the authority of the clergy to perform their functions is divinely conferred; but equally clearly this authority is exercised within the whole company of those who participate in Christ.

We have tried to confine ourselves to ways of speaking about priesthood which are true of it 'in itself', and so to distinguish it from the various sociological roles which it is called upon to play. At a time when, in many parts of the world, these roles shift rapidly and men find it hard to adjust, it is all the more important to hold the essentials clearly and distinctly. We have also confined ourselves to discussion of priesthood in the general sense which we began by outlining. This office is amply held by the bishops and priests of Catholic Christendom, though in them and in all others it is impaired by the disunity of Christians, which prevents its bearers from acting unhaltingly as the sacraments of God's perfect charity. We have deliberately refrained from using the term to refer to the second of the three traditional orders of ministry and from discussing the issues raised by that narrower application. Priesthood is essentially a function (or a group of functions) which many different kinds of Christian clergy exercise, including many who are (with considerable justification, given the muddles which Christian usage has provided for it) reluctant to use the word to describe it.

It may seem that at a time when even the case for the worth-whileness of religious inquiry has often to shout loud for a hearing, the doctrine of priesthood is only of the most peripheral importance. But Christian faith is never happily divorced from Christian life, and it is hard in practice to have much experience of the Christian religion without being confronted with the Christian ministry. It may be important for a man to know how to think of it quite early in his contact with Christianity. He may need to know, for example, what kind of authority the clergyman carries. A man may even meet the priest before he knowingly meets God at all, and if at that stage he cannot be expected to understand the priest's significance, at least the priest himself ought to know whether his priesthood signifies much or little, and precisely what.

### Note

1. So much so that there is sometimes a sense of mystification when this proves difficult. See, for example, *Conversations between the Church of England and the Methodist Church: A Report*, Church Information Office and Epworth Press 1963, p.23: 'A measure of theological uncertainty or disagreement as to the intrinsic nature of the priesthood of ordained

ministers and its relation to the priesthood of the laity or of the whole Church is not intolerable, and is not incompatible with the establishment of communion between our two Churches or with fellowship in one Church.'

# 9

# *The Worth of Arguments*

It is a matter of deciding what arguments are good for what. We can easily think of cases where a coherent argument is presented to us but we fail to be convinced. Of course we may be struck by blind prejudice, so that no *argument*, of whatever power, would move us. But we may be more praiseworthy than that. It may be that the argument used just does not strike us as having force for the purpose alleged. Satisfactory within itself it may be; but it remains a self-contained entity. It has no power, as far as we are concerned, to go beyond itself to demonstrate the necessity of the steps which are urged.

For example: an advocate of present-day Conservatism may draw up a case showing beyond a doubt that in the last thirty years of the nineteenth century the policies adopted by Conservative governments were more beneficial for the economic life of the nation than those adopted by Liberal governments. The figures prove it, he cannot be gainsaid. The argument is complete within itself, and, left at that, it is valid. But supposing that he then expects us without further discussion to turn out and vote Conservative at the next election. We may fairly retort that his argument leads to no such conclusion. We should say, broadly speaking, that much water has flowed under the bridge since 1900.

Of course, given one condition, we might well be impressed by his efforts at persuasion. If, in addition to our capacity to see the force of statistical historical arguments, we were endued with a powerful sense of tradition and institutional continuity, this might make us impervious to those who pointed out that English politics now were not exactly like English politics then, and we should vote as the Conservative advocate desired.

We might move from one position to the other. We might begin by finding the argument from tradition irresistible. It carries automatic conviction for us. Disraeli and Salisbury were, in respect of England's prosperity, markedly successful prime ministers: it cannot but be right to support those who share their label and wear their mantle. Then our mental set may change. It is not exactly that new arguments have come our way; it is rather that the whole shape of the question has changed for us. Mr Heath calls himself a Conservative, as Disraeli did; but what of that? We are in the 1970s. The men, the problems, the policies, the conditions are all vastly different from those of a century ago. The mere continuity of a name is but one element in a picture of enormous complexity and cannot by itself lead us to such conclusions.

In theology as in politics (and other spheres too), there is difficulty in knowing what *worth* can be properly set upon various kinds of argument. There is also the more intractable matter – that, even with the greatest goodwill, it is often hard for those who find one set of conclusions inescapable to understand why others find them not so in the least and are mystified by what they consider to be unjustified leaps to conclusions. In an area where not only zeal and fervour but also piety and reverence are involved, it is all too easy to fail to be aware of the situation. The result is that theological discussion is often barren (even where there is a genuine search for agreement by those who begin by differing), because it takes place at the wrong level. It does not begin by analysing the criteria and laying bare the method. Yet it is at this fundamental level that both harm – and good – must effectively occur. Here clarity may be made or marred.

Of course much that passes for the subject matter of theology (and in some cases has done for centuries) may need to establish afresh its title to be considered in that category. Indeed, this is one of the questions on which mental set may alter – for a person or a church or a culture. There is again a partial parallel in politics. Certain matters important in any discussion of constitutional questions a century and a half ago would now scarcely figure on the agenda and would be replaced by others: e.g. the monarchy and the bishops in the House of Lords would occupy less space than the trade unions and the party machines. Yet it would not be impossible to find people to give continued weight to the old issues because of their traditional place in the country's constitutional arrangements; and in attending to them at the expense of the newer institutions they might appeal to 'the British Constitution' as a quasi-mystical thing, in which no formal change had occurred to take account of either the unions or the party machines. Others would dismiss such an approach as refusal to face current realities.

The question of the proper range for theology is akin to the question of what arguments count for what. For 'theology' will have different agenda, depending on the source used. If scripture, then much concerning God and Christ, little on the precise structure and institutions of the church, less still on conservation and abortion. If tradition, at its maximum, then a vast range of matters, to which Christians have at one time or another devoted thoughtful attention – far too many to handle usefully. If the scholastic method, then a relentless sequence of related questions: that which demands treatment once the process of orderly argument has been entered upon. In these days of economy and retrenchment, when theology must be not diffident but careful in staking its claims, the range of theology may be just what the name implies – that which can be said about God, neither more nor less; and its interests may best be served by caution in moving outwards from that powerful centre. If such movement takes place, let it be certain not to lose the aegis of the centre. So we may investigate the implications of what is said concerning God for this or that matter of proper Christian concern: and that will be the way of tackling the theological task. One policy will be unsatisfactory – yet how people hanker after it! That is, to attempt to gather nosegays of theology, according to their interests, from the results of different ways of setting up its agenda – this from scripture, this from the councils, that from the speculation of Aquinas – each in its own terms, or perhaps all seen from a vantage-point foreign to them all, that of some brand of modern man.

So far we have not mentioned the ordination of women. But we have sketched the world of discussion in which the matter should be argued. What then are the arguments and what are they worth?

If the theological and ecclesiastical present is to be determined by the theological and ecclesiastical past, then the ordination of women must fight hard for a hearing. A medieval abbess or two behaving episcopally do not make an argument. And clergy-women are hard to find in the New Testament, though there is room for discussion about equivalents between then and now. Indeed, here is an argument not dissimilar to our example concerning the Conservative party. Undoubtedly Christian congregations in New Testament times had male leaders, and though women played a prominent part, formal leadership cannot quite be ascribed to them – and there are arguments brought against it (e.g. I Cor. 11.3ff.; I Tim. 2.12). Undoubtedly most Christian congregations still have male leaders. But, before we look at hypothetical females, what about those male leaders? and those congregations? There is continuity, yes; there are similarities in activity – the message and the rites. Yet may that continuity not be counteracted by the great differences between the circumstances of society and the church then and now? by differences in the role and activities of the men involved? And if the details of male ministry may not be unquestionably derived from the New Testament, not only because they are partly obscure but also because it is not clear how (let alone why) they should now be reproduced, with what force is it possible to claim to leave women for ever in the position they occupied in those congregations in Greece and Asia Minor so long ago? It is the naïve confidence of the positive claims to reproduce New Testament states of affairs in this regard or that, which saps confidence in the usefulness of the negative claims, i.e., the rejection of what cannot be discovered in the sacred text. The same sterile, unhistorical quality attends the idea of giving permission to women to be clergy as long as they are not congregational leaders (on the grounds that in New Testament times they had quasi-clerical functions but not the rule of churches). By what logic exactly can then lead so precisely to now? Here it is not just a question of carrying conviction; it is a matter also of hard realities: by what criteria are the church of the first century and that of the twentieth comparable? Is it to be seen as a matter of totting up continuities and discontinuities? What on earth is the value of that? Yet how otherwise can we find enough continuity to allow enough identity between the two for our common Christianity to mean anything? We may be on a more promising path if we look rather at the shape of belief concerning God and see where we are led.

There is no plain sailing if we would find today's judgments in such matters in the behaviour of yesterday, including that of New Testament times. And we shall find no argument there for the ordination of women which will not give us more headaches than it relieves; even if we shall not find any knock-down argument against it either.

But Christian history has one lesson for us, one which in recent decades has increasingly pressed itself on the alert Christian consciousness, often to its discomfort. It is the degree to which Christian ideas and institutions have been continually in flux, adapting themselves to changing conditions, even at the price of manifest inconsistency with their past. Is it then beyond the limits of Christian adaptability to ordain women when their social position is so vastly changed? But this is no theological argument, merely an observation from history.

Perhaps there are other ways of doing theology, of formulating theological argument, which deserve consideration. Let us take it that Christian theology consists of saying what can be said concerning God as disclosed in Jesus and encountered in the Christian experience. Pure theology, that is, concerns God. The rest is comment, extrapolation, application. It is the attempt to see how a matter is to be judged in the light of that powerful centre. So the 'theology of the ministry' is the attempt to map out the implications of Christian understanding of God for the matter of the church's ministry; and the question of women's ordination is one aspect of that.

But does the light of the powerful centre truly shine that far? Is not this matter on the very edges of theology? If we put the approach in more personal terms and ask, 'What is God's will in this matter?', can we for a moment suppose that he wants us to do anything other than use our common sense? If social institutions point that way, if there is need, if there is desire, let not 'theology' be falsely involved. It has no bearing on the matter, at least not in the way of solemn, elaborate argument. It is a matter of expediency for the church, no more, no less; that is the level at which judgment must be made.

Yet from the powerful centre the light of God shines powerfully, and he who numbers the hairs of men's heads and without whose knowledge sparrows do not fall takes seriously the institutions by which his gospel is proclaimed. There is not an item in all creation which may not speak, to the attentive observer, of the Creator. And if we do not so attend, how can we know him, how can we be in the way for 'doing theology'? The method is symbolic, and the glory of symbolism is appropriateness. In this language, Jesus is what he is for us because he is the superbly appropriate symbol of God. Not (let us say hastily) by his maleness, but by his teaching, by the nature of his death and his new life, by all that has flowed from him. The priest of the church too is a symbolic figure and it is best if the symbol is as complete as possible – many-sided and appropriate.

But symbols only 'work' if they communicate their significance. They may do it in ways that are easily explicable: the priest symbolizes Christ as he presides at the eucharist. They may also do it in ways which those who 'see' can barely express even to themselves – indeed they may be hardly aware of it, though it may be crucial in their lives. So the priest, in all sorts of intricate ways, often symbolizes fatherhood, with many complex strands; and people may love or hate him for it, for reasons beyond their control. If a symbol does not not communicate, and the skill to use it cannot be revived, it may as well be abandoned.

Symbols are not the heart of the truth they express, though they commonly gather the affection that belongs to the truth itself. So when they fail to communicate, there should, ultimately, be no serious regret – provided the valuable truth is not lost. This is the reverse side of our remark about the capacity of everything to speak of God. Everything can speak of God, but when and whether it will do so is a secondary matter, changing with time and place, as social conditions and sensibilities change. What matters is that God should be heard!

So the question is: if the priest, is, in various respects, a symbolic figure (representing now Christ to his people, now God to the world, now his people to each other and to God), is maleness essential to his appropriateness, his ability to communicate what he stands for? And if it is, is it so at the articulate level or only at the inarticulate? If indeed maleness were in this way essential, then no doubt the cause of women's ordination should be seen as a piece of doctrinaire theorizing. But this is a case for testing consumer reactions. However powerfully fitting in theory the maleness of the priest may be alleged to be for his symbolic effectiveness, that case will fall if this is not sensed or understood by the faithful. There is nothing sacrosanct about symbols – though people should no doubt be heartily encouraged to explore those that are central. What matters is that the truth concerning God should be perceived; and if female priests can now, over whatever range of comprehension, facilitate that appropriately, what hesitation should properly remain?

In one respect at least – and it is a matter of theology – this appropriateness must surely be admitted. Right at the beginning of Christianity, St Paul expressed the insight that 'there is neither male nor female, for you are all one in Christ Jesus' (Gal. 3.28). He meant that with regard to what God had revelaed, accomplished and provided through Christ, men and women were on the same footing. His words are not a licence to Christians to eradicate as many distinctions as possible between the sexes in every area of life. If, however, we see his statement as a proper expression of the central Christian convictions, then Christian institutions ought to express it wherever possible. In our earlier language, the symbolism of these institutions ought to cohere with the message. It can hardly be denied that women priests would be an appropriate form for that symbolism to take. On the other hand, this argument, applied to this particular aspect of Christian life, would not overtop all arguments from expediency; it is not 'hard', mandatory theology, for the working out in human life of the implications of belief in God cannot so easily be formulated or decreed. It is, rather, an option which is open to us if circumstances make it desirable for the proclamation of the gospel so that it may be heard.

There is an odd contradiction in the Catholic tradition which bears on this matter. One Catholic tendency is to make the most of symbols – it is the sacramental principle, and it is, for reasons such as those outlined, extended widely. But with regard to the priesthood, there is another tendency which works in the opposite direction. Not the personality of the priest but his priesthood – that's what matters. The man is rendered anonymous by his role, signified, for example, in his vestments as he stands at the altar. The unworthiness of the minister does not invalidate his priestly acts. It is odd that those who have used this approach do not always find it easy to envisage that anonymous bearers of priesthood might be women. Perhaps the women would not necessarily take kindly to such a tepidly welcoming argument!

# 10

## *On the Grace of Humility*

The Rev. William Master endowed this sermon in 1684; and he left to his preachers the choice of some dozen texts, mostly from Proverbs or St Paul. But he did not forbid us to use additional texts, and I propose to take advantage of that omission. In deference to William Master I choose I Corinthians 1.23, 'We preach Christ crucified'; and of my own volition Psalm 116.13, 'Right dear in the sight of the Lord is the death of his saints.' The first is to hang as a backcloth to my whole sermon, the second is to get me launched.

'Right dear in the sight of the Lord is the death of his saints.' One view of the history of Christian thought is that it has moved from one issue to another, one controversy to another, one crisis to another, each arising in a particular set of circumstances, each expressing the needs and interests of a particular age. As the focus of attention shifts, that which riveted the minds of one period fails to excite the interest of another; and it becomes something of a mystery that people once felt so much fury about the matter in question. But from another point of view, Christianity never lays the ghosts of the great crises of its past. They live with it, seemingly, for ever. Perhaps ghosts provide too shadowy a metaphor: better say that however the pattern of Christian thought develops and shifts, those crises are woven into it and refuse obstinately to disappear. So it is a commonplace that the early Christian expectation of a speedy end of the world has remained undigested in Christian theology from that day to this. Christians have continually found ways of dealing with that expectation at the level of piety and practice; but reflective theology has never quite come to terms with the renovation of belief demanded by the failure of the world's end to arrive. The strand persists uneasily in the pattern.

But early as that crisis was, there was another still earlier. It was the death of Jesus. The precise shape of the crisis of faith which it caused eludes us: we have no immediately contemporary evidence. But one thing is clear: Jesus was the source of a many-sided and most vivid reordering of his followers' understanding of God, their relationship with him, with one another and their neighbours – of their whole setting in life. And Jesus was dead, the vision was threatened. Even if the understanding he had conveyed could take martyrdom in its stride or even hinged upon it, still there had to be adjustment to the fact.

The belief in Jesus' resurrection was, in a sense, the simple answer, the neat resolution of the crisis. It reversed the death, erased the element of defeat. But from the first, Christian theology chose not to concentrate on that path alone, but rather to attend to the death of Jesus itself and explore its sense. So began that endless fascination of the Christian mind with death; that constant readiness to find in death the key to living, in self-abandonment the path to self-discovery before God, in poverty the only true wealth. The crisis of Jesus' death, which the resurrection might have resolved for ever, at a stroke, thus remained. From that day to this, Jesus' death has stood at the heart of Christian consciousness – partly a proclamation, but partly an enigma, the occasion of a crisis of faith if not on the surface then just below it; demanding an account of itself, upsetting any faith which sees itself as smooth loyalty to a benign God, forbidding complacent religion, rebuking mere moralism – in effect, the fertile source of that vitality in Christian faith which refuses to let us rest in our convenient compromises with God and our consciences.

That early crisis still haunts us. No, it does more. Without that strand persisting in the pattern of faith, without that point of constantly renewed fascination, the Christian identity could scarcely be maintained.

Christian theology has been in league with historical study for a long time now. But only recently and only in some quarters (which is partly a periphrasis for Oxford) has it admitted historical study to the citadel of its heart. That is, it has come to acknowledge its own dependence, for the shape and colour of its thought, at any given time, upon the culture within which it lives. It has come to see its own solemn utterances as part of history, and therefore as volatile, flexible, adapting themselves to their environment, even when reacting strenuously against it. This heightened awareness of the chameleon-like quality of Christian theology, this franker acceptance that it is not immune

from the common circumstances of human thought, is shared by
the few, resisted by the more who have heard about it and dislike
it, and undreamt of by the many who, in so far as they consider it
at all, see the Christian faith as an unchanging rock in an uncertain world, thereby confusing it with the God whom it proclaims.

On 13 February 1976 the Church of England moved a step
towards recognizing the legitimacy of this awareness in the publication of its Doctrine Commission's report on *Christian
Believing*.[1] The report did not enjoin this way of believing, but it
did recognize its Anglican existence. Writing in the issue of 12
February, the Religious Affairs correspondent of *The Times*, who
is a Vatican II Roman Catholic, perhaps revealed the limitations
of that great Council in his comments upon the Doctrine Commission's report. In disclosing the mobile and varied nature of
present Anglican belief, the report provided, so he felt, an insufficient body of doctrine to serve as a basis for the church's mission. He failed to appreciate part of the message of the report –
that is, how mobile and varied Christian doctrine has been in the
past and how the belief in fixity is itself a culturally conditioned
phenomenon rather than a simple historical judgment. The
church's mission must surely rest, not on that which will prove
acceptable or striking to a particular audience, but on that which
is true – including that which is true about its own character.
Whatever the character of Christian belief, with that character
believers must reckon to live.

I offer two reflections on this approach to Christian believing,
which, as a signatory of the Doctrine Commission's report, I can
hardly deny to be one way of looking at it. One reflection quali-
fies, the other exploits the approach I have described.

First, despite the relativism which bites deeply into almost any
attempts to discover absolute continuity of belief and concept,
there are certain deep-seated features of the Christian consciousness, which, however overlaid, however variously expressed, remain in being. Pre-eminent among them, no doubt, is
what Paul saw as preaching Christ crucified and what I have
identified more dialectically as a constant worrying at the fact of
Jesus' death and so at the theme of death itself. Amid all the shifts
in Christian belief and sensibility, you could present that worrying at death, that continuing memory of Christ's death, as the
perpetual crisis of faith, which continually stimulates the Christian and delivers him from the complacency of his own self-
generated religious ideas. It makes God problematic: for how can

the Creator God be discerned in a death? and how can I live satisfactorily under the banner of death? That is, what kind of life can find its focal point of interpretation in death? This is a God who defies interpretation in terms of mere theistic speculation. He is a God who reduces us to the silence of worship.

But also, at a more personal level, it makes God both intelligible and welcome. For only a God somehow to be interpreted by a death and the precarious exposure thereby implied can be a God who is close to humankind. Only such a one can be my God. And only when God embraces and comprehends death can life this side of death be neither a burden nor a mockery. Such a concentration on death is the condition for freedom from essential anxiety now. This is not because any suffering short of death will then seem light by comparison. It is because a belief in God which plays upon his involvement with death, a faith that death cannot separate us from the love of God, gives fresh proportions to everything else. If death is in God's hand, I can love my mortal companions in life without the dispiriting sense that death is the ultimate threat to love. No, death is the creature of love, not its master. If death is in God's hand, I can accept the events in life which diminish and disappoint me. I can even embrace them because by failure I have tasted that which alone leads to life. I have been forced to abandon that illusion of private immortality which success gives. Yet there is no dark puritanism here: for to focus on death is to find freedom unanxiously, both at the level of belief and at the level of practical spirituality.

Christian humility at its purest always drinks directly from the fount of Jesus' death. It springs spontaneously from life seen in the light of death. It easily degenerates into caricatures of itself: into acceptance of place in a hierarchy, fear of presumptuous interference with things as they are, or reluctance to disturb accepted belief and practice. Yet all these vanish like mist before that genuine humility which smiles at death as the friend and agent of God's love.

The second reflection is this. This humility which I have described affects every aspect of Christian life, not least the business of stating and propagating the Christian faith. Sometimes, humility meets plain and palpable enemies – such as the crude pride which is the subject of this sermon's ugly sister in Michaelmas Term. But on the theological front, the enemy is more shadowy and is disguised in the armour of light. Christian theologians and contemplatives have always recognized the futility and sheer unfittingness of speech about God. What can be said that will not do more harm than good, mislead rather than instruct, present the preacher rather than his God? Yet how can the thoughtful adherent of revealed faith be silent? And is it not perhaps a matter of how the words concerning God are to be spoken and how they are to be heard?

The man at *The Times* was baffled and shocked by the Anglican theologians because they spoke with varied voices and not as, for example, popes are, by long habit as well as by conviction, inclined to speak. But perhaps Christianity has by now tried the firm loud voice for long enough and needs the strength that comes from diffidence where diffidence is fitting. It sounds like a policy born of caution and uncertainty. It had better be born of attachment to Jesus' death. 'We preach Christ crucified.' Part of his death was the death of his living voice. His words ceased. They were henceforth, those fragile things, at the mercy of human memory and human pens. Himself, he left no writing, no words of his own to sound directly in our ears. And just as his death as a whole was the seed-bed fertile for the renewal of faith, which reflected the rich variety of those who believed, so the death of his voice was the signal for endless diverse attempts to speak of God in his name. In practice, the words continually changed in tone and content, seeking first this way, then that, of giving terms to the experience of which he was the cause. And even while avowing fixity and stability, Christian thinkers adapted their message to new audiences, so that, by all means, the gospel could be heard. That diversity has been the condition of hope realized, love made known, heaven brought to earth.

The time may have come for us to embrace more warmly the death of Christian words as the condition for revitalizing the message. The intellectual tool is the recognition, born partly of theology's walk with history, partly of theology's own convictions about God, that the words of faith are provisional and approximate. But deeper than that is the religious conviction, that those who preach Christ crucified must extend their humility to the very formulation of the gospel by which they live. This application of the lesson of death to the content and not merely the superficial manner of our witness has hardly begun to penetrate the official Christian mind. But the cost of the blank hold on life, and the refusal to embrace this death, may be the imposition of a death of a much less creative kind.

Our embracing of death, in so far as we can achieve it, is dear to

God because it enables us to live with him by faith; and that is the path of mature relationship with him. Only the man who can see death as God's gift is ready to receive the death-like experiences of life as occasions of grace. His humility will be the well-spring of his freedom and his strength. If only we could dare to bend our words when we speak of God, in the faith that he may be heard through us! If only he were not muffled by our determination to suffer no death of our precious religious words!

By such means, the manners of theology, spirituality and ethics may flow into a healthy unity. So that we consider, adore and serve one God who bids us to rise to him in the freedom of friendship, in the wonder of his grace.

William Plomer wrote:

> Everything bends
> to re-enact
> the poem lived,
> lived not written,
> the poem spoken
> by Christ, who never
> wrote a word,
> saboteur
> of received ideas
> who rebuilt Rome
> with the words he
> never wrote;
> whether sacred,
> whether human,
> himself a sunrise
> of love enlarged;
> of love, enlarged.[2]

## Notes

1. *Christian Believing: the Nature of the Christian Faith and its expression in Holy Scripture and Creeds*, SPCK 1976.

2. From William Plomer, 'A Church in Bavaria', in *Celebrations*, Jonathan Cape 1972, and reproduced by kind permission of the Estate of William Plomer.

# Index of Names

Abraham, 26
Acts of the Apostles, 20
Adam, 45
Africa, church in North, 10, 93
Alexandria, church in, 7
Antioch, church in, 10
Augustine of Hippo, 18, 24, 78, 81
Augustus, 15

Brown, Peter, 24
Bucer, M., 76, 86

Calvin, J., 75f.
Clark, F., 83
Clement of Rome, 69f.
Couratin, A. H., 82
Cranmer, T., 76, 86
Cross, F. L., 83
Cyprian, 71f.
Cyril of Jerusalem, 73

David, 15
Deuteronomy, 70
*Didache*, 69
Disraeli, B., 105f.
Doctrine Commission, 114
Dutch Reformed Church, 19

Ephesians, writer to the, 54
Erasmus, D., 74
Ethiopia, church in, 10
*Exultet*, 17

Farrer, A.M., 37, 39

Hamerton-Kelly, R.G., 51
Heath, E., 106

Hebrews, writer to the, 21, 31, 55, 78f., 94, 98
Herod, 15
Hezekiah, 17
Hippolytus, 86
Hodgson, L., 32, 39
Hopkins, G.M., 48, 52

Ignatius of Antioch, 8f., 16f., 24
Irenaeus, 69–71
Isaiah, book of, 14, 31, 69

Jeremiah, book of, 69
John, gospel of, 31, 46f., 55f., 78, 94
  epistles of, 55, 73
  Revelation of, 21, 31, 94
Josiah, 17
Justin, 69f.

Kee, A., 41, 51
Knox, J., 52

Lambert, J.D., 83
Liturgical Commission, 59, 84
Luke, 46

Maccabean martyrs, 10
Malachi, 62, 68f.
Mark, gospel of, 67, 69
Mascall, E.L., 83
Master, W., 112
Matthew, gospel of, 7, 25, 46, 54f.
More, P.E., 83
Muir, E., 48, 52

Nicaea, Council of, 30, 33